Adam Meets Eve

Foundations for Love to Last a Lifetime

By Peter A. Kerr

*All God's best,
in all your relationships!*

Peter A. Kerr

ISBN-13: 978-0-9899698-0-2

Cover design by
Andrew Kerr at
RelevantStudios.com

The Buzz about *Adam Meets Eve*

Adam Meets Eve as a book proposal won a "Top Three" award out of more than 250 submissions from the Tyndale ReWrite Conference in 2012. Since then many more people have been saying kind things, some of which have been captured below.

"Peter Kerr's book, *Adam Meets Eve*, is a fresh, new look at tested and true principles on relationships, courtship, sexuality and marriage and brings us back to a solid foundation on which to build our marriages, families and society! A must read for 'marrieds' and all who desire to be in this lifetime committed relationship."

> **-- Greg Williams, Director of the Kentucky Marriage Movement and Co-host of the weekly TV program *Marriage Unleashed***

"As I began courting the man of my dreams we read and discussed this book together. It opened the door for us to talk about important topics and figure out if God wanted us to become husband and wife. Out of all the books we read about relationships before we were married, this one was by far the most helpful and challenging."

> **-- Kimberlee Brooks, Newly married recent college graduate**

"Based on sound research and personal experience, Peter Kerr's *Adam Meets Eve* is a compelling read that calls me to a deeper relationship with my spouse that is God-honoring and fulfilling because it is centered on servant leadership rather than self-centered pleasure. Very practical, this is also one book I can hardly wait to purchase for my teenage daughters since it will prepare them for life-long commitments in marriage. I believe this book can profoundly impact the thinking of our generation that desperately needs a Biblical paradigm for marriage in the midst of a sex-crazed culture."

> **-- Luke Kuepfer, Lead Like Jesus Seminar Speaker**

To the One True God of Love

I dedicate this book.

May He use it to glorify His name and build His

Heavenly love into our earthly relationships.

CONTENTS

1. Why Adam Needed Eve: Foundations of Relationships   8

2. A Suitable Helper: How to Attract Anyone Worth Attracting   31

3. Would you give up a rib? How Attraction Develops into Intimacy   53

4. It was Good: What's Love and Is There Just One Right One For Me?   76

5. Tree of Knowledge: How Do I Know I'm in Love and How Far is too Far?   96

6. Male and Female He Created Them: Gender Equality and Leadership   126

7. Adam Isn't Eve: Communication and Biological Differences   145

8. Flowers, Figs or Fur Coats: How to be Romantic and Communicate Love   168

9. Talking in the Garden: Essential Dates and Discussions   196

10. Knowing Good Fruit from Bad Apples: Marriage or Break-up?   222

11. And There Was Light: Small Answers to Big Questions   247

12. Endnotes   274

FORWORD

The Bible says that, "among many counselors is great wisdom", so I have endeavored to recruit many people to help this project be the best it can be. Every little bit of encouragement, every scrap of constructive criticism, every word of caution from my many draft readers has helped make this book possible.

First, a quick note on terminology. I intentionally chose to write "gender" where "sex" is more accurate to designate male or female. I realize "sex" is the correct biological word, but I feel it is too confused with the action in our culture. For the same reason, I avoid using "lover" and instead speak of an intimate other as "paramour," hoping to express the idea of "one you love" and avoid the connotation of "one you have sex with."

Just as no man is an island, so no book is the work of a single person. I'm grateful to more people than I can name here, but let me at least acknowledge a few sources of inspiration. First, I want to thank my wife Rebecca for her shining example of what a loving spouse should be, and for allowing me to make our personal story known to many. I also thank my four wonderful children Asriel, Mikiah, Zachary and Saraya who graciously sacrificed time with me so I could write this. You inspire me to create a better world for your future, and I feel privileged to be your daddy. Appreciation is also due to my family of origin, who first taught me what a loving family can be. Thank you Philip, Mary Ann, David, Stephen and Andrew Kerr.

This book would not be nearly as good without the support from the great people at Asbury University. Thank you to Dr. Don Simmons and Dr. Steven Hillis for mentoring me in the ways of teaching communications. Thanks also to Ben and Maria and all the kind folks at Brannon Crossing Panera – now you know why I hang out with you so often! Thanks to Lisa, Esther, and the rest of the folks at The Fedd Agency for believing in the book and making way for it to win one of the top three best book submissions in 2012 at ReWrite.

Many students and other people read the draft, encouraged me, and made the book better. At the top of the list must be Melissa Landon who edited the book and Janah James who assisted with social media marketing—you both should be at the top of any employer's list, and I hope to work with you again on future projects. Thanks also to Stephen and Kimberly Brooks, Paul and Stacie Landess, Luke Kuepfer, Kelsey Adams, Elijah Friedeman, Joshua Friedeman, Anna Houben, Tim Eastridge, Kendall Igleheart, Caleb Mootispaw, Lauren Timmons, Rachel Dery, Joel "Cato" McKenzie, Kelsey Adams, Ruth Jeffers, Mike Rosecky, Rosie Cooper, Jeff Wagner, Tim Vaughan, Jennifer Crowell, Ellen Worsham, Jason Parmer, Jason Gillilan, Shannon Greiwe, and Stacey Attig. I probably forgot to name a few, so in general thanks to the many people at Asbury, Church of the Savior, and around the world who asked about the book, offered suggestions, and anticipated its arrival. Thanks for the hours of draft reading and editing and sharing with me ideas that have immeasurably improved the book. I, of course, claim responsibility for all its defects. May God bless you all, even as you have been such a blessing to me.

All the best in all your relationships,
Peter A. Kerr
September 2013

CHAPTER 1

Why Adam Needed Eve: Foundations of Relationships

"One word frees us of all the weight and pain of life: That word is love."

- Sophocles

I was free. At 22 I graduated from the US Air Force Academy with a degree in engineering and a degree in psychology with emphasis in leadership and was commissioned as a 2nd Lieutenant. After a brief vacation I moved to Washington State, where I worked for the Air Force and started serving as a college/career pastor at my local church. I was free in another way too. Having dated the same lovely lady for five years, I finally realized God was not calling me to marry her, so we experienced a peaceful if somewhat reluctant breakup. I was now an eligible bachelor.

I was excited to be out on my own, making a decent wage, and leading people both at work and in the church. God had gifted me with preaching skills, and I loved coming home and being alone to read a book or do Bible studies preparing messages. If I wanted companionship, I simply set up an event for the college/career group we named LIGHT (which stood for Living In God's Holiness and Truth). People from LIGHT were over at my house three or four days a week, often on the pretext that we'd watch a movie, but I don't think a single movie was ever shown. Instead, we'd sit around discussing the wonders of God, the ways we could minister to people, and other relational subjects.

As a carefree 22-year-old, I remember being totally in love with God. His presence was sweet and fulfilling, and my love for Him easily drowned out the typical temptations of being a young man in America. I would study the Bible and pray for hours, asking my Father in Heaven many questions and pondering the purpose of life. While some of my mental meandering was so that I could teach my weekly Bible study, much of it was simply the desire to know more about God and myself. Though it may seem strange to others, I was rather content, and I asked God why I should get married, why I should love one person in a special relationship, and why I needed anyone else when I already had the fullness of God.

I knew the Bible speaks approvingly of staying single (see Paul's wise advice in I Cor. 7:7-9), and though I naturally was attracted to women, my passions were in check, and I probably had the will power to stay single for life. At the same time, I doubted I actually had this gift of singleness, simply because I didn't **want** to be single for life but instead found the idea of marriage and raising a family very appealing. I guess while the passions were in check, they still existed. Wouldn't God alleviate the desire for marriage if it were His will for me to remain single?[1]

After work one day, I was in a particularly intimate moment with God when a question struck me. Why did Adam need Eve? After all, Adam had the fullness of the loving Father, enjoyed perfect communication and cooperation with God, and was surrounded by the paradise we call the Garden of Eden. Without Eve there may have been no sin and fall, though I'm pretty sure Adam would have found a way to mess things up all by himself. In any case, why did the first man still have a need when He enjoyed the fullness of God?

As God often does when I boldly approach His throne, He told me I was asking the wrong question. If this were a human conversation, I may have given up right there. But I didn't, because this wasn't, and I knew that the answer to this question was critical in my own journey toward understanding relationships. God had something very profound to teach me, if only I would persist in thought and prayer. So I thought and prayed.

It took two days of thinking about it before it suddenly came to me. For me, asking God the right question is often half the battle. Instead of asking the more self-centered question that was on my mind, I had to ask about Him and what was on His mind.

So I approached the throne of grace again, and this time I asked why He created Adam. After all, God exists without need, in complete communion with His eternal self, the community of the Trinity in perfect unity and harmony. The universe seemingly would have been better off had God simply entertained Himself with other matters instead of creating mankind. Why did the all-sufficient God of love decide to create humanity?

The answer came quickly this time. I sensed God say it was because He loved so much that He had to give it away. It was not an imperfection in His character, some sort of unfulfilled need, or even a desire to be entertained by observing the human race. No, in His perfection, the perfect Giver had to have a receiver to share Himself with. Love is perfected only when it is given.

Thus humanity was created. I had the answer to my original question, too. For you see, Adam was created in God's perfect image and was living without sin as a reflection of God on earth. Adam had the same desire that God did. He had so much love that he desired someone to be a recipient of his love. And so Eve was created, the perfect love accepter and reflector, generating love in kind and shining it back on her mate. For love is a strange thing in that, contrary to the laws of physics, it expands and grows when it is reflected. In Eden, love originated from God, built momentum in Adam and Eve's relationship, and was reflected back to God in a perfect circle of increasing love.

The first sin ruptured this relationship of love and created a division between humanity and God. It also divided men and women, and it is to this remarkable event that we now turn in order to better understand how men and women now struggle to relate to each other.

The Fall and its consequences in relationships.

There are many solid analyses explicating the story of the Fall, so we will not go into detail here except as it reveals something about the relationship between men and women. It is quite possible that Eve was never told by God not to eat of the tree of good and evil but that she received her instruction from Adam (Adam is given the command in Gen. 2:16 before Eve is created). If this is the case, then Eve's first act of disobedience was against man as much as against God, and the first direct disobedience against God falls squarely on Adam's shoulders. Furthermore, the Genesis story recounts that Eve ate the fruit in the presence of Adam "who was with her" (Gen. 3:6), suggesting Adam was giving his consent to the sin and maybe was just being a coward and seeing how it affected Eve before he, too, followed his disobedient and deceived heart.

The silence of Adam is deplorable, as is his blame-shifting when challenged by God to give an account for his behavior (Gen 3:12). The summary of the story suggests not that Eve, and subsequently all women, is to be blamed for the sin, but that both Adam and Eve shared the culpability and passed to their offspring a similar propensity to sin, often called "sin nature" or "original sin." Furthermore, both men and women are cursed for their disobedience, and here is where we can see many of the roots of tension between the genders.

"To the woman He said, 'I will greatly increase your pains in childbearing; with pain you will give birth to children. Your desire will be for your husband, and he will rule over you.' To Adam he said, 'Because you listened to your wife and ate from the tree about which I commanded you, 'You must not eat of it,' Cursed is the ground because of you; through painful toil you will eat of it all the days of your life. It will produce thorns and thistles for you, and you will eat the plants of the field. By the sweat of your brow you will eat your food until you return to the ground, since from it you were taken; for dust you are and to dust you will return.'" (Gen. 3:16-19, NIV)

There are a few different interpretations of verse 16, but the most straightforward explanation seems to be that women are cursed to "desire" a husband who will "rule" over them. Sadly, men have historically lived up to their end of this curse, often "ruling" over women in degrading and sometimes even abusive ways. It has only been in the last century, and only because of a strong Christian heritage of freedom, that the fundamental value of women has finally been recognized and true equality of value to include voting and legal rights has been recognized for women.

From an interpersonal perspective, men may lord it over women precisely because of fundamental differences in the genders. Women tend to have a greater need to be married, and have greater personal interaction requirements/desires. Interpersonal communications theory sheds some light on Eve's desire and consequent subservience, as it postulates that the person who cares the least for a relationship is in effect in control of the relationship. In his book *Too Soon Old, Too Late Smart* Gordon Livingston writes, "Any relationship is under the control of the person who cares the least." He goes on to say that the person who cares/loves the most experiences a more euphoric high but also feels out of control in the relationship. This person must constantly give in to the other's desires because they need the relationship more. Giving repeatedly and selflessly opens them up to more and more pain should the other reject them.

Livingston's theory doesn't presuppose that it is always the male who loves less, but most data suggests men need conversation less and do not require as much relationship maintenance activities as women, again suggesting men will be more controlling in relationships. In any case, it seems incumbent upon men to alleviate some of this curse by refusing to use the woman's desires against her and instead to be a servant leader who controls the relationship only because he legitimately wishes to give more than he takes. We'll look more into what it means to have servant-leadership in chapter six.

The partner who cares/loves less in a relationship typically feels guilt about not loving as much but still ends up in the driver's seat as they get their way and call the shots. This leads to skewed control and authority dynamics, and often it's a seed of argument and discord. I believe the partner who loves less also compares their love to the other person's, and this creates more doubt about the relationship's future as they wonder if maybe they don't love enough since they don't love as much as their partner.

The partner who loves more also must endure difficulties. This partner typically keeps needing affirmation and constantly wonders if the other person really loves them. Such doubt can lead to cloying behaviors and other actions that do not make them more appealing but instead can lead to relationship termination.

Obviously the perception of unequal love leads to a continued spiral of disintegration. The most healthy relationships must therefore be based on both people loving/caring fairly equally or both willing to give selflessly and be "out of control" for the other. This is one reason love is so hard to evaluate or measure, because it was made in its purest form to be absolutist: to really love is to love completely, and if both love completely selflessly, then both love equally.

Some truth about men's struggle in marriages can also be gleaned from this Genesis account of the curse. Adam is told that the earth is now cursed and that he will have to toil to make it yield its produce. It must have been magnificent before the Fall since all of nature gladly provided for the human caretakers of earth. On my honeymoon in Maui, one of the Hawaiian Islands, I caught just a glimpse of what this must have been like. The trees on the island flowered in radiant colors with blooms that would put most roses to shame, and when the wind blew, petals would gently float down on couples strolling along the beaches. Other trees bore huge fruit that made the branches heavy, causing them to lean down to about eye level as if offering people their tasty refreshment. In Eden, humanity didn't have a worry, and the natural world they were placed there to safeguard and cultivate worked with them instead of against them.

Anyone who has been bitten by a mosquito or had weeds crop up in a garden recognizes those idyllic days are long past.

People can hardly enjoy nature without bugs or itchy grass or sting weed getting into the picture. Nature was humanity's servant, but the servant is now out of control. Mankind therefore began a long process of harnessing nature, striking it with plows, manipulating it with tractors, and finally putting the full force of science to the task with modern chemicals and biological treatments.

Striving to subdue the earth, though mentioned specifically in an agricultural context, surely also means that man's lot is to work hard throughout his life rather than continue to enjoy Eden's leisurely pace. Humans have proven up to the task and today have succeeded in ameliorating the worst of many of the Genesis 3 curses. For example, drugs help women at childbirth, technology applied to agriculture has created an abundance of food in industrialized nations, and women have finally been granted equal rights and liberties in many modern nations (most notably the ones that have a Christian heritage).

The psychological effects, however, seem to linger, since husbands often put work ahead of wives and children, and money has become one of the main points of contention in relationships. Men often have difficulty balancing the time they work for the family outside the home with their parental responsibilities in the home and struggle to build positive relationships with their wives. When it is the woman who works outside the home, this particular issue tends to be less of a problem. Women seem better capable of making the family a priority rather than bowing to the continued siren song of needing to work longer hours. However, many women end up frustrated and complain that though they wanted to "do it all," they don't enjoy having to do all the work both in and out of the house.

Women have been placed in a particularly difficult position in our society because they seem to get the message that they can't be fulfilled if they are "just" a wife and mother, but at the same time they understand they will not be fulfilled without *at least* being a wife and mother. Often the career alone path looks less enchanting at around thirty years old as the woman's biological clock starts ticking. Additionally, women are increasingly having to take a more serious role in wage earning because males either won't or can't provide for the whole family. This leads many women into the error of usurping the male leadership role rather than submitting and working together in a partnership as the Bible portrays.

We'll discuss roles in marriage later and especially the role of servant leadership, but here we are concerned with how men and women often balance needs differently, possibly due to the curses meted out after the Fall. Baxter's Relational Dialectics Theory[2] proposes that people have powerful needs that are polar opposites, and that people have to keep rebalancing them in order to be satisfied. For our purposes the internal dialectics are most important. They can best be described in the chart below:

Internal Relations Dialectics:
    Autonomy vs. Connection
        (balancing Integration and Separation)
    Openness vs. Protection
        (balancing Expression and Non-expression)
    Novelty vs. Predictability
        (balancing Change and Stability)

The first dialectic is the need to balance autonomy and connection. All people want to be autonomous, having the freedom and means to do what they want and be different from all others. This is a repelling force because it has to do with wanting to be singled out from the crowd and not labeled. Often our autonomous drive can be seen in everyday distinctions such as wearing unusual clothing or having a unique hairstyle. Westerners, with their highly developed sense of individualism, are naturally repulsed by people all dressed the same or housing developments where all the houses look identical.

We also want to be part of a group to find a place where we belong. The connection dyad is an attractive force, drawing people into groups and communities. We want to gather with people who are similar in some way, ranging from worshiping God in the same manner to sharing chess as a hobby. To connect with others means lack of differentiation; instead, the emphasis is placed on conformity and sameness. Obviously, these two polar opposite desires exist in us but cannot be simultaneously satisfied.

As one would predict based on the Genesis 3 curses,

women typically have a stronger connection need whereas men have a stronger need to differentiate. This is probably why women are better at putting the family as a higher priority than work. Men want to succeed at work so that they can be special, differentiated from others, which may lead to sacrificing the family for achievement at a job.

What is really ironic is that even the man's desire to differentiate often occurs precisely because he wishes to be part of a group. Men strive hard in sports so they can be recognized individually, but the purpose of this striving is so they fit into the team's pecking order. Men stay at work longer than they should because they wish to get ahead, typically so that their colleagues will respect them more. The drive to be autonomous and gain fame is actually the male's way of trying to fit into the collective.

This dialectic has a parallel in the nature of God. Though the word "Trinity" is never mentioned in the Bible, the concept is found from cover to cover, as Genesis uses a plural form of "God." The book of Revelation even more clearly shows the triune God at work. The Trinity describes how God is one but reveals Himself in three persons; God the Father, God the Son, and God the Holy Spirit. These three persons have always existed in perfect harmony, forming a sort of community. Of all the characteristics of God, this one may be the most difficult to fathom, yet I believe even its qualities are ingrained into the human psyche as humanity was made in God's image.

Possibly this Trinitarian nature is the cause of the Autonomy-Connection dialectic. Humankind strives to be like God in His Trinitarian form. We wish to be perfectly united to others yet remain perfectly ourselves. We want to be perfectly transparent and infinitely known, but at the same time we strive for distinction and separation—to be individual and unique. Within every one of us rages this struggle to be known yet remain a mystery, to be open and disclosed but still completely loved. We want intimacy, but we also want individuality. We crave company but we also need time alone. Somehow we are incapable of perfectly imagining God's nature on this variable, which might be because God's nature is only possible with the help of undiscovered powers or dimensions. String theory in physics predicts that eleven dimensions exist, so the members of the Trinity could be both more "united" and more "individual" than we could ever imagine.

Like colliding billiard balls, humanity seems to race head-on into one another, only to bounce away again when the conversation gets too deep or the pressures too great. Sometimes the collisions hurt and leave discoloration on our personalities that affects future encounters. Often our balance between the paradoxical forces of pulling together and pushing away is disturbed, so we put up fences to ward off others and protect our vulnerable hearts, or we seek others all the more desperately, hungering for acceptance and recognition.

The solution to this paradoxical dialectic was also created in the Garden of Eden. Even as God designed humanity with these raging desires in conflict, He provided a way to work out our longings. His solution is the magnificent gift of marriage. Within marriage both partners lose themselves, and possibly in that loss find themselves all the more complete. The two partners give of themselves, and somehow as they sacrifice themselves they are redefined as one that is greater than the parts. Marriage is where husband and wife can both completely "autonomate" as well as connect. Aristotle once said, "Love is composed of a single soul inhabiting two bodies."[3] In many ways this book is about learning how to connect with someone else, how to not simply bounce off but actually engage with someone, and how to build a bridge between two souls that will last a lifetime.

One further note is necessary here, as some may note that long-term singles (those who are gifted with singleness) can achieve a satisfaction in this area. Christianity has long suggested that this is the case because in effect the single person (historically nuns and priests) are in a way "married" to God, and thus derive from Him directly their satisfaction of the autonomy-connection dialectic.

I believe every person who is single should drink deeply from the well of God's love and presence so that they are mostly satisfied on this dimension and not compelled to marry. This was my providential experience, since I could have chosen to marry my girlfriend of five years but instead trusted the Lord's guidance and correctly ended that relationship, trusting God to meet all my needs. While that long-term girlfriend was an excellent person and a joy to be with, had I married her, I would have missed out on God's highest plan in the next lady I met—Rebecca—whom I eventually courted and married.

When are you ready to look for a mate?

Many people think that dating starts at fourteen to sixteen years old and that age alone is a good enough criterion to decide when a person is ready to start searching for a lifelong partner. While we'll discuss the purpose and practice of dating and courting later, let me briefly differentiate the two terms by saying that dating involves trying to get to know a person, whereas courting involves seeking to know someone for the explicit purpose of possibly marrying them. While dating is also discussed, here we are mostly concerned with what factors should be considered before one starts courting (seeking a husband or wife).

When people establish a minimum age for dating, typically the intent is to ensure that a minimum level of maturity is present. In our family, a minimum age of sixteen years old has been established before any of our four children may date. However, just turning sixteen will not qualify anyone for dating. Since age does not perfectly correlate with maturity, a more subjective measurement will be applied after fifteen to determine a child's eligibility. For anyone wanting to date, the difficult question is: "What are the attributes of a person who is sufficiently mature to start dating?" Since a dictionary definition of "maturity" results in circular logic for our purposes (maturity is the end of an age or when something is fully developed or grown), it makes more sense to define maturity in terms of attributes that must be present before a person is ready to date.

One obvious attribute of maturity is independence, i.e., the ability to do something without assistance from others. An immature person depends on elders for assistance, whereas a mature person can navigate all normal obstacles on their own. This attribute is certainly reflected in the common initial dating age of sixteen, which happens to be when a young person also gets a driver's license and thus achieves a greater independence than ever before. Sixteen is far from a fully mature age as these teenagers are still wholly reliant on their parents for money, shelter, and many other essentials of life.

Independence alone, however, is certainly not maturity. There are many immature people who are independent. Complete independence is both impossible and undesirable because we are supposed to grow more toward dependence on God and not less. Indeed, while mature people are independent in many areas, they also tend to better grasp the extent of their dependence in other areas. A mature person is big enough to admit need for others, strong enough to risk relying on others, and wise enough to ask for help (unlike the 2 year old whose mantra is "I can do it by *myself*," even for tasks that are too difficult for him or her).

From a psychological perspective, maturity has to do with adaptability and responding appropriately to an environment. It refers to a response that is learned rather than instinctual and includes knowing the correct time and place to behave in an appropriate way. People need to know when to be serious and when not to be too serious, when to laugh and when not to laugh, when to take offense and when to shrug off a comment. Without this kind of maturity, relationships tend to be more destructive than enjoyable. With this kind of maturity, even the relationships that seem destructive can become instructive. Maturity brings many benefits, smoothing interpersonal relationships and often resulting in rewards from society.

While this type of maturity may be considered a

prerequisite for teenage dating, something more is really needed before a person is ready to find their lifelong mate. A further type of maturity is the ability to love. Love means putting someone else before one's self and being willing to sacrifice and hurt for another person. In my mind, the quintessential characteristic of maturity is the ability to spend one's self in protection, love and benefit for another. Thus, the perfect symbol of maturity would be a God willing to sacrifice Himself for His creation.

I remember playing in the forest as a teenager and coming across a bird. I was thirteen, and our yard opened up into a huge forest where I had constructed several forts. I was in the process of reconnoitering a site for another fort when a small bird burst out and flew right at me. I ducked and then quickly swiveled around to see if it would attack from behind. The bird instead landed abruptly and then skidded across the earth as if it were wounded. This made little sense given the speed and agility I had just witnessed. I took a few steps toward it, and it skittered away a few more yards, still hopping on the ground as if unable to fly. I pursued it a few more feet, trying to get a look at its wing and wondering if it had been hurt. I hoped I had not been the cause of its distress. After leading me on for about thirty feet, the bird suddenly took to the sky and disappeared.

I returned to the spot I had been when the bird first appeared and pulled back some branches. Snuggly tucked into a low nest were some baby chicks. I only had a few moments to look at them before the parent bird swooped in at me again and once more tried its feinting maneuver, attempting to lure me away from its chicks. This bird was ready to sacrifice itself in an effort to protect its offspring.

Maturity involves being able to see that some things and other people are more important than self preservation. Just as a mature bird will sacrifice herself for her chicks, a mature person is willing to sacrifice personal reputation or possessions to assist others. A mature person has, first of all, a solid foundation from which to give of the self (is financially independent, emotionally stable, etc.) and secondly has the inclination to assist others. Such a person can lose a game and not feel too bad, knowing someone had to lose and being comforted by the fact that someone else won and feels good. Such a person can give up their meal for another person, or their comfortable seat on a bus for the elderly. Such a person is ready to give and thus mature enough to consider marriage.

Marriage is never about taking but is instead about giving. All too often the dating game is played by two people who have holes in their hearts, with deep-seated needs that were not filled in childhood. These people seek someone who can meet their needs, who can make them feel whole. Often these type of people find each other and create unions based on filling the holes in each other.

Such unions are undermined from the outset. People should not come together because they have a need to take, but should instead only begin seeking a lifelong relationship when all they have is love to give. Like God who had so much love that He created Adam to be a receptor of love, we are not ready to enter a lifelong intimate relationship if we are not fully whole in ourselves and therefore in a stable position to start giving of ourselves. This is why it is silly to start courting at a young age, when the self is still forming and individuals harbor many insecurities and have many interpersonal needs.

The Apostle Paul clearly thought getting married was a distraction from serving God completely, and therefore suggested that everyone consider the option of being single for life.

> "Now for the matters you wrote about: It is good for a man not to marry. But since there is so much immorality, each man should have his own wife, and each woman her own husband. The husband should fulfill his marital duty to his wife, and likewise the wife to her husband. The wife's body does not belong to her alone but also to her husband. In the same way, the husband's body does not belong to him alone but also to his wife. Do not deprive each other except by mutual consent and for a time, so that you may devote yourselves to prayer. Then come together again so that Satan will not tempt you because of your lack of self-control. I say this as a concession, not as a command. I wish that all men were as I am. But each man has his own gift from God; one has this gift, another has that. Now to the unmarried and the widows I say: It is good for them to stay unmarried, as I am. But if they cannot control themselves, they should marry, for it is better to marry than to burn with passion." (1 Corinthians 7:1-9, NIV)

It is vital that young people consider Paul's words carefully. The apostle sees great blessing in being single and even considers it a gift. We must fight our culture's bias toward marriage and honestly try to understand if this is a gift we have. Certainly we all have this gift for a time before marriage, and we must use that time wisely, investing it by building our knowledge of God and relationship with Him.

The excuse Paul gives for marriage is that people "burn with lust." This might be a good indicator that you do not have the gift of celibacy. On the other hand, far too many college students rush into marriage as the cure to their "burning" rather than controlling their passions and temptations. I'd estimate that only half the "burning" is natural—the other half is caused by our culture's preoccupation with sexuality which fans the flames of temptation. We'll discuss how to fight that temptation in chapter 5. Here it is important to note that it is much wiser to stay single longer and resist temptation than to rush into a premature decision to marry.

Paul does not deprecate or forbid marriage, but he warns us that pursuing a mate takes time away from pursuing God. *This leads to the primary prerequisite of dating or courting; before you seek a romantic relationship, you must enjoy an excellent relationship with God.* From one's faith comes the maturity level required to court and be married. From spiritual discipline arises the strength of character required to love and sacrifice. We learn from God a kind of love that is complete, overflowing, and totally unselfish. Marriage was meant to be built on that kind of foundation.

One day after work, I returned home and prayed a dedication prayer to God, telling Him I wanted to live my life for His glory and that I was willing to give no matter how much in order to gain no matter how little of Him. I had not been dating for a few months, and I told God I was willing to be celibate for life if that was His desire. I told Him that if He wanted me to marry, He'd have to arrange it because looking for a mate was distracting and difficult to separate from being lustful. Just as the Kings and Patriarchs in the Old Testament arranged marriages for their children, I told God He would have to arrange my marriage. I was not even going to consider a lady unless she showed up at Bible study or flew out of the sky onto my doorstep. I wanted to give God a supernatural option, which would make it even easier for me to discern the lady was the right one.

God seemed pleased with my prayer but responded with a challenge. I felt I was being asked that if just one more person would come to a saving knowledge of Christ due to me being single rather than being married, was I saying that would be my preference? I know it sounds selfish, and I know the eternal life of one person has far more value than all the banks on earth could hold, but this concrete example really hit me hard. Was I really willing to sacrifice being married for a single soul? For a hundred souls, maybe, but for just one? I had already led many people to Christ by that age, so I knew something of the joy that involved, but I found it hard to compare one more soul to the joys I desired from marriage (and, to be honest, the joys I expected from a sexual relationship, since by God's grace I was a virgin then and remained so until I was married).

I struggled for two weeks in prayer over this issue, but I finally realized I had said I'd give "no matter how much." It was with true resolve that I accepted God's challenge and agreed that if it were His will, and even if it were for only one additional soul, I would remain celibate. I told God this wouldn't be my first choice, but I also reaffirmed that I would not seek a romantic relationship until He led me to the right person.

Three months later Rebecca was a newcomer to the Bible study I was leading, and the Holy Spirit said as clearly as I have ever heard Him: "She's the one for you." I thought "Wow!" because she was knock-out gorgeous, but my response to God was: "Thank you, but please help me not to be distracted by her from preaching your Word tonight." I was then given the interesting task of falling in love and courting the woman I knew I would marry.

Funny enough, Rebecca had also recently made a pact with God, but hers was a bit different. She had decided the normal dating dance wasn't working for her, so she promised God five months of just dating Him. This decision is obviously right in line with Paul's teaching about the merits of singleness. Ironically, it was when both of us had given up on conventional means and decided to just trust God and seek Him that He fulfilled all our desires and helped us meet each other.

We have seen this same pattern repeated over and over again during the last 16 years we have ministered to the college/career age group. The principle seems to be this: You are not really ready to get married until you are ready to be single. When you have surrendered all and are ready to accept whatever God wills, then He often goes over and above and beyond all expectations!

CHAPTER ONE FURTHER LEARNING

1) Learn more about relational dialectics on the Internet. Consider where your balance point is right now on each variable. Do you swing back and forth quickly or do you tend to be more often on one side? Would it be better to find a mate who is similar to you or who has opposite tendencies?

2) Read Genesis 1-3 and think about how men and women get along. Try to create a theory of your own grounded in these scriptures.

3) What does being made in God's image mean? Could it mean more than one thing?

4) What does God mean when He says "the two become one flesh"? How does this practically effect a marriage?

5) Do you agree that one reason God made humanity is because He has so much love He wanted an object for that love? Can you think of other reasons God created humanity?

6) Are you ready to start seeking a lifelong partner? What should you do in your life to start preparing for that special future relationship?

7) What qualities of Christ do you think are essential to have in your future mate?

CHAPTER 2

A Suitable Helper: How to Attract Anyone Worth Attracting

"Dating is trying to be someone you aren't in order to impress someone you don't know." — Anonymous

How do you attract anyone worth attracting? Pray. Okay, that's not a very surprising nor satisfying answer, and it isn't my total answer, but it certainly is part of the answer. I prayed every day since I was 11 that God would protect and lead me to the lady I would marry. My mom prayed for the wives of all four of us boys even before we emerged from the womb. Prayer is essential to discovering God's will, and no amount of other wisdom can replace that fact. However, there is more to the answer, and more you can do to attract the right person to marry.

Getting the spouse of your dreams will not be easy, but with God all things are possible. In fact, there are many things we can do to advance this goal. I often advertise seminars for young adult audiences by announcing "I will give you the secret of attracting anyone who is worth attracting." While I risk some people considering the audacity of such a claim and deciding to stay away, over the years I have gathered large crowds and typically have very satisfied "customers" when I'm done. There is indeed a secret to attracting the opposite gender, and quite a bit of research that reveals what people find attractive and are looking for in a mate. This chapter looks at why we are attracted to people, what women are looking for in a man and what men are looking for in a woman, and yes, will eventually reveal my proven secret for attracting anyone worth attracting!

Attraction Characteristics

Many factors thought to be the cause of interpersonal attraction have been proposed and studied. While we can certainly decide whether or not to act on our impulses, for the most part attraction is not a choice but is a function of five main factors: physical attractiveness, familiarity, similarity, complementarity and reinforcement. We'll therefore start by looking at each of these factors.

Physical Attraction

The fact that good looks make us more attractive hardly astonishes anyone, but what is surprising is exactly *what* we think is good looking. We all have an idea of what is beautiful or handsome. We could probably establish some general criteria of what it means to be attractive, though even there we'd have some disagreement. The level of disagreement would increase in direct proportion to the diversity of our backgrounds.

Physical attractiveness is highly susceptible to cultural definition. People in Mexico and South America view pale/white skin as desirable, whereas many Americans and Canadians pay good money to spend hours "fake baking" at tanning salons. Upper-class women in the 17th and 18th centuries used parasols to keep the sun off their skin, thinking darker skin suggested a lowly field worker and was unfit for rich maidens. Chinese ladies today also use parasols, not because work is beneath them, but as one lady in Beijing told me, "I do not wish to get dark and ugly".

This cultural definition shows up on many more variables, challenging what we think is pretty. Most of us would readily identify with the Greek standards of beauty carved into statues of gods and goddesses. These show men with well-defined muscular builds, strong noses and cheek bones, and women sporting hourglass-shaped curves with ample breasts and hips on an overall slender frame. Most of us would therefore be surprised to see a Viking goddess statue from the dark ages, with large hips, a few hundred extra pounds, and fairly fleshy faces. Even their chief god, Odin, hardly seems well-fit with a fleshy face and a beer-belly. The Viking standard of beauty for women included large birthing hips and extra weight so as to better weather their cold winters, and only successful wealthy men could afford the food and mead necessary to generate well-rounded bellies. In many of the earth's poorer countries extra pounds are still envied for signifying wealth.

If we created a list of characteristics to define attractiveness, and then used our criteria to rate various people's attractiveness, we'd find ourselves applying the criteria differently. We'd probably also discover that while the ratings on a 1-10 scale are close (only a few points off) indicating a general agreement about what is attractive, there would be enough variation to support the notion that we have individual "tastes" in looks.

Interestingly, even our tastes are impacted by our culture, or at least by those around us. If we think others believe a woman is good looking, we will reevaluate and raise our opinion too. Brain scan studies show that the reward centers in the brains of young men looking at photos of young women vary based on learning that their peers thought a particular woman was more or less attractive than they did originally. This effect isn't just peer pressure, as their brains actually adjusted the "value" of the face and the biochemical response associated with it[4]. Thus just setting up an expectation that someone is good looking, such as by starring in a block buster film, will make that person actually seem to be more attractive.

Science also can help us understand what most people consider to be attractive physical features. Studies have shown that we like about an eye's length of space between a person's eyes, and that we prefer good facial symmetry (if you draw a line perpendicular to the nose through the nose we like the two sides to be mirror-reflections rather than have different proportions). Furthermore, our "tastes" may be influenced by our own faces, as studies confirm we are attracted to people who look like us and have similar attitudes to our own[5]. If you ask me this is even more true as we age, as I have noticed many older couples seem to start looking like each other (and even acting like each other). Even more astonishing, it seems we are attracted to people of similar attractiveness, as we typically marry people who are within one point of our own attractiveness rating on a ten point scale[6].

Perhaps the most astonishing fact of attraction is that we are not attracted to a special set of outlying characteristics that few people have, but instead we are attracted to average features. The more average features you have the more attractive you are. Langlois & Roggman (1990)[7] tested this theory using 192 scanned photographs of male and female Caucasian faces and then using the computer to create composites of each image (2 faces melded together, then 4 then 8 etc.). The original faces and amalgamation faces were then rated for attractiveness by 300 judges on a 5-point Likert scale (1 = very unattractive, 5 = very attractive). The results showed that the photo composites of the most faces (32 faces) were the most visually attractive. While this is great evidence to conclude that we like average (not sub-average or super-average) facial features, I don't suggest you tell your girlfriend or boyfriend "you are truly average-looking!" and expect positive results.

There are of course other features that effect physical attraction. In one of my public relations classes I had students give a questionnaire across campus that discovered the number one trait a guy must have to be attractive is that he showers daily. This factor eclipsed theological beliefs, "being hot", and even personality. Step one appears to be being clean, a feat most of us can accomplish with minimal effort.

A little more effort may be required to maintain a healthy weight, but this too is very much possible for nearly everyone. Every year I ask the guys in my classes what body shape they find most attractive, and I get the same answer after a little deliberation: males are attracted to a healthy body weight, not the ultra-skinny model often parading on television and movies. If skinny is your natural weight, that is attractive, but if you are naturally a plus size or somewhere in between that is attractive too. The truth is, men like women who are at a healthy weight for their own bodies, and women are not necessarily attracted to the body-builder male stereotype so much as appreciate a well-toned physique.

All these studies on physical attraction should not make anyone feel unattractive as much as hopeful. It turns out that just about anyone can be physically attractive if they take care of themselves, maintain a healthy weight, have a good diet, and practice solid hygiene habits. You do not have to have some sort of outstanding physical characteristics to be attractive, but instead you only require average characteristics, and most of us have at least some of those.

The other good news is that physical attraction is rather temporary. While it is a powerful initial attractor, other factors seem to be more persuasive over the long term. This is a very good thing, as physical beauty typically peaks in the late twenties while there is still potentially 60 years or so of marriage left in a relationship. Physical beauty is nice to have when you are young, but no one gets to keep it forever, so it is much better to marry someone for characteristics other than physical beauty. We now turn to more internal characteristics that are attractive, which instead of waning with the years actually can strengthen over time.

Familiarity

Another universally accessible attractiveness variable is familiarity. It turns out that we are attracted to people with whom we spend time. The more you are around someone the more comfortable you become with them and this can lead to liking them. I'm pretty sure this is why my mother likes me— she was around me for 18 years straight!

C.S. Lewis writes about this type of attractiveness in his book "The Four Loves"[8] where he explicates the Greek word "storge" (στοργή) which is translated "affection" and is defined as fondness through familiarity. Lewis describes *storge* as the most natural kind of love because it is present without coercion, and it is the most widely diffused because it is indiscriminate, paying the least attention to other characteristics deemed valuable. We simply spend time with someone else and they sort of "grow" on us and us on them. In my mind this is a wonderful kind of attraction, because it is one force that serves to strengthen long marriages. Another way to look at this attractiveness variable is to consider that maybe the longer we are around a person who is beautiful on the inside the more capable we become of seeing the full person and allowing the inner beauty to color the outer frame.

One caution may be needed here: just because familiarity

grows attraction in general it does not mean you should become a stalker. Sure, signing up for a college class with a potential paramour may be a good idea, but signing up for all the classes she has and sitting outside her dorm everyday may prove a bit much. You cannot force people to love you by being around them more, but you certainly need to at least be around them enough for them to recognize you and hopefully develop a relationship with you.

Similarity

We are attracted to people who are like ourselves. Philosophically this makes sense, but it is also possibly the root of racism. Most likely our subconscious reasons as follows: "I like myself and I am not dangerous to me. Thus, if someone is like me they have a better chance of liking me and also not hurting me. Therefore I will like people who are like me". This way of thinking of course leads to us favoring people who are similar to ourselves, and often even making false assumptions about entire people groups based on trivial facts such as that their skin color is not the same as ours.

I have not been immune to the tendency to like people who are more similar to myself. I'll never forget the first young lady I had romantic feelings for at a Christian camp. She was a high school senior and I was just a sophomore who had been allowed into the junior-senior camp week. She was a cute and spunky 5-foot tall blonde who completely dazzled me with her larger-than-life personality, deep spirituality, and I'll say it, great looks. We "did the camp thing" and held hands for two days followed by a flurry of letters after camp to include exchanging pictures. The funny thing is, everyone who saw her picture wanted to know if she were my sister. Even when I said "here's a picture of the girl I met at camp" people would think themselves funny by asking "you dated your sister?"

Years later I married Rebecca and had a similar experience. On our honeymoon we were asked if we were brother and sister. Before that question I had never even thought about a similarity in appearance, and even now I confess that while we shared some similar features, she was certainly a lot prettier than I ever was!

While my camp and honeymoon experiences are examples of similar physical traits being attractive, this category of attraction is much broader than just the physical. Indeed, we like people who see the world the way we do, who believe in God the way we do, and who like to do the things we like to do. Anthropologist Helen Fischer found that most people date and marry someone who is similar to themselves in physical attractiveness, financial background, intelligence, and values[9]. Botwin, Buss and Schackelford (1997) discovered that although individuals differ greatly in the personality characteristics they desire, they still prefer mates who are similar to themselves. While women tend to have much longer lists of desirable traits in a mate, both men and women generally succeed in obtaining mates who embody the characteristics they most desire[10]. I always think this study is funny because I never made a list of desirable traits for my mate, whereas my wife had a list of more than 60 traits she wanted in a man (and she prayed God would grant her such a man!). While I'm sure I don't live up to all her expectations, she has assured me that she feels the prayers were answered and that I meet at least her most important qualifications!

Complementarity

Some may have read the last category and thought "but I thought opposites attract"? Actually, that is true as well, and is captured in this category that says we are attracted to people who are different than ourselves in key ways. While we are attracted to people who share essential characteristics with us, we are not looking for clones, and we like to be surprised by people. In many ways we are attracted to people who balance our personalities or somehow "complete" us which involves being diametrically opposite to us.

As suggested in Chapter One, the reason we get into relationships is to find someone to marry, and the reason we marry is to be more complete (balanced) and thus able to be used more by God. I believe that my wife Rebecca's work for God as an individual plus my work for God as an individual is greatly exceeded by our work for God together as a couple. We support each other, and experience synergy in our ministry and balance in our personalities. Thus you want to marry someone who really has differences from you. Ideally you'll marry someone who has a different personality type from yours, different spiritual gifting, and even a different birth order (first born, middle born or last born, all of which we'll discuss further in Chapter 10). The more differences in these types of variables the better chance you'll be able to balance each other out and create synergy in your ministries and family.

Perhaps one reason we like complementarity is that we can

learn from others only when they are different from ourselves. When people hold a different perspective, and we honestly care about them, we are willing to check our own assumptions and rethink issues. If "just anyone" disagrees with us, we tend to discount their opinion in an off-handed manner. However, if someone we like is different we're interested and so will explore the difference in an attempt to understand them better. In that process, we will most likely also come to better understand ourselves.

I think "complementarity" is also fueled by the essential differences that exist between men and women that pull us together like opposite magnets. In my classes every semester I put gals on one side of the room and guys on the other to discuss their differences and list what they find most difficult about the opposite gender. After some honest and often comical and awkward conversation, I end the class by asking "if you could change something about the opposite gender, what would it be". I am not surprised when both genders come to the mature conclusion that even what frustrates them about the opposite gender is attractive, and that they wouldn't change a thing.

I believe part of "complementarity" is that men find the differences between men and women to be simultaneously tantalizing and frustrating. Men are like lions on the hunt, and they want their prey to challenge them. Women are naturally finicky as well, often not understanding their own emotions which results in unpredictable behavior that men marvel at. Men will say they just want a women to be straight-forward, but if you look carefully you'll find guys often do not date the women they understand and can talk to easily "as a friend". Instead, part of the motivating force to court is found in curiosity, and we are curious about the things we do not understand and that are different from ourselves. We'll look much deeper into this phenomenon and other factors effecting male-female communication in Chapter 4.

Reinforcement

Reinforcement in this context doesn't have the military meaning of bringing in back-up forces, though often in a relationship you wish you could have some good advice and support fast. Instead, reinforcement here means that we are attracted to people who give us something, whether tangible or intangible, that we value. We like to be rewarded for being in the relationship, and benefit from spending time with someone. In its most base form this includes the desire to date people who take us out to eat and give us gifts, most typified by Madonna's "Material Girl" lyrics which state in part:

They can beg and they can plead
 But they can't see the light, that's right
 'Cause the boy with the cold hard cash
 Is always Mister Right, 'cause we are
 [Chorus:]
 Living in a material world
 And I am a material girl
 You know that we are living in a material world
 And I am a material girl...
 Some boys try and some boys lie but

I don't let them play
Only boys who save their pennies
Make my rainy day

Intangibles may also reward us, as dating a certain person can raise your popularity or soothe the psychological damage done by the last breakup. More common (and noble) intangibles that reinforce our attraction to someone include intellect and humor. Maybe we like to learn things and our date is full of interesting facts, or maybe they tell a lot of jokes to make us laugh (not only an enjoyable experience, but also helping tighten our abs).

Humor is a double "reinforcer", as we both like people who are funny and enjoy it when our companion laughs at our jokes. Laughter may be a very powerful indicator of how much someone likes you: I always felt if I met a lady who not only got my puns but enjoyed them I'd have a winner. I was blessed with marrying a lady who not only gets my intellectual humor, but can crack the puns back at me, greatly reinforcing my attraction to her.

What Women Really Want in a Man, and What Men are Seeking in a Woman

The father of English literature Geoffrey Chaucer (1342/3-1400) once wrote "Women desire six things: They want their husbands to be brave, wise, rich, generous, obedient to wife, and lively in bed."[11] That would indeed be a tall order, since in typical female fashion some of the characteristics are a bit incongruent. For example, it may prove difficult to be both rich and generous, or wise and brave, and it certainly would be hard to be all these things and remain blithely obedient. After years of observing couples and counseling them, I think Chaucer might have been on to something, but I wouldn't agree with his entire advice.

Indeed, I think I have narrowed what women are really looking for in a potential mate down to a single word. While my answer is certainly not comprehensive, it is the closest single characteristic I believe every women is looking for in a future husband. Furthermore, when I reveal it each semester in class all the ladies seem to sagely shake their heads in agreement, confirming my guess may indeed be the key ingredient that makes a man desirable.

Strange as it sounds, I think women are looking for maturity. Maturity means adulthood or being "grown up", and is characterized by knowing oneself (which leads to confident humility) and living a life of balance. A mature man has achieved balance in head and heart, work and play, action and contemplation, passion and repose. Socrates once remarked that we should be grateful to old-age because it allows passions to rule us less, yet we should also realize that no passion means no great purpose in life. The mature man exudes confidence with humility, respect for others but also respect for himself, and makes people feel safe and at ease in his presence.

What women really want is a man who is comfortable with himself, so much so that he is in a position to sacrifice himself or his own glory for others. Women don't want boys but want to be with a man who has gentle strength, tempered passion, and enough greatness to be humble and generous to others.

This type of man doesn't act brash like youth and isn't easily offended, and he certainly has enough humility not to pulverize an athletic opponent and then rub it in. Indeed, a man who can take defeat graciously is much more attractive to ladies than a boy who wins and tries to bask in his own glory. Maturity means having life-wisdom, being emotionally-developed, and having a sense of independence.

This type of maturity is attractive because it is exactly what a lady needs in a long-term relationship. Women don't need men who are selfish but seek husbands who are willing to sacrifice for their wives and families. Women require men who are self-confident and can protect them and create an environment of shelter and comfort. A mature man will not just follow his lustful desires but will remain faithful, having made a mature decision to love rather than getting into a romantic relationship only for personal gain. We'll discuss exactly what a mature decision to love means in Chapter Four.

Though I am reluctant to admit it, I watched "the Bachelorette" once and saw this principle in action. The bachelorette on her first date with a guy (we'll call "Steve") was excited when Steve said that though he is 30, he is really a boy dressed up like a man. Steve meant this to inspire curiosity and pique the bachelorette's curiosity, which it succeeded in doing. However, three weeks later the bachelorette was looking for a life-mate, and so she questioned Steve again about his initial comment. Thinking it worked well the first time, Steve confirmed his boyish nature. He was sent home that night without a rose, and with the bachelorette explaining that she was not looking for a boy but for a mature man. While youth has energy and initial attraction, maturity is like gravity that continuously pulls us toward a person and can keep relationships together.

The search for maturity is probably also why women date men who are 2-3 years older. While "youthful", "good-looking" and "energetic" are all attractive qualities, ultimately a women needs a guy who will "settle down" with them in a meaningful, stable relationship. They need someone who has personality depth so that they can connect at a level deeper than just physical, and women will reject the boy with a superficial personality often constructed from cultural cliché and self interest. Women want a man who can give and not just take, and often this ability stems from a core of maturity.

This hypothesis also helps us understand why it often seems that nice girls date "bad boys". The proverbial "bad boy" mimics maturity in that he goes against the grain in a way that seems self-confident and independent. Unfortunately, his self-confidence is typically a facade created to hide his inner core of self-loathing, and his independence is not a mature ability but originates from a rebellious temperament that is extremely self-centered. Having seen many of these kinds of relationships, it seems to me that they are typically short-lived as the young lady quickly discovers her mistake. However, the lady often just stumbles into another similar relationship because she is often incomplete herself, craving attention and self-worth from any male. Typically the lady's real problem relates to having a rotten relationship with her father, as good fathers create positive self-esteem in their children. Men tend to compliment accomplishments making children feel capable, whereas mothers more often love unconditionally making children feel valued.

Strangely, these days males are extending their period of immaturity, which is in part responsible for pushing back the average age of marriage in the U.S. In 2009, men's first marriage was at 28.4 years old on average and 26.5 for women[12] . According to the *Atlantic*, men used to mature because they were forced to work, which meant developing discipline since they had to do something that they essentially didn't want to do. Work teaches self-sacrifice and discipline, as you have to give up immediate pleasure for the sake of future pleasure (or at least future sustenance). These days childhood and joblessness is often extended well into college-age and beyond, and boys are more busy playing video games than learning to relate with women. This is resulting in most women not even considering 50% of men as serious potential mates, increasing competition for mature men and often making college-aged women date men who are well beyond college age.

Men are also failing to mature because they seldom have a good father-figure at home and certainly do not see mature men in the media. Masculinity has been attacked in the last few decades not just by the hyper-feminist movement, but much more by the constant bombardment of negative stereotypes in movies and on television. In nearly every sitcom the father-figure is the brunt of the majority of jokes and is portrayed as stupid, lazy, disconnected, and lorded over by his wife. Men are confused as to what it means to be masculine, what it means to lead like a man in the family and workplace, and where the line must be drawn between chivalry and chauvinism, or emotional sensitivity and emotional weakness.

Furthermore, evidence suggests that boys who are raised without a proper father figure do not tend to be effeminate, but indeed over-act the masculine traits they see on television, treating women poorly as objects and tools instead of as equals. Fathers are often not growing up because they are abandoning their responsibility to raise children. Research reported in the *Scientific American* (2011) suggests that fathers sprout supplemental neurons and experience hormonal changes after the birth of a child[13]. With few examples of what mature masculinity means, and a propensity to abdicate their responsible role in society and families, it is no wonder that women are having a difficult time finding mature males.

I'm sure women also want to know the secret to attracting male attention, apart from the obvious "look like Brooklyn Decker" (a tall, trim, blonde movie star). Strange as it may sound, I find it much more difficult to explain what men are seeking in a relationship. This is because there really are many different answers, and because most men don't know themselves enough to know what they are seeking. This foolishness of not exploring one's own desires often leads to simply dating or courting because the man is physically attracted, and can result in the guy marrying mostly because he wants to consummate the physical relationship rather than because he has carefully selected a life-long partner.

If I had to boil it down to one characteristic, I would say men are essentially seeking beauty. This is often confused in the male psyche with just seeking external beauty, which is the easiest to find and pursue, though wise men will eventually discover that outward beauty alone is unsatisfying. It takes much more effort to discover inner beauty such as the character described in Proverbs 31 and I Peter 3:3-5, but once revealed it is an even more powerful attractor. Men want to hold someone who is kind and who exudes goodness—they want a delicate flower they can protect and nurture. Men want to marry virgins who are pure and possess an inner quality of great beauty.

Many women cater to the folly of men overemphasizing the external beauty and do not spend enough time developing their inner beauty. Paradoxically, the lady who spends an exorbitant amount of time worrying about her external beauty reveals that she may be less lovely inside (since she is consumed with outer appearance), and a lady who is beautiful on the inside is often not considered for dating because she doesn't spend enough time making the exterior attractive. Most guys I know do not like women to use very much make-up, and prefer a woman who can "let her hair down" to a woman who has to always look perfect. Men will often discount a lady who always must look "perfect" because they realize she is most likely "high maintenance" (i.e., she would require too much continuous effort, typically in the form of emotional support or putting up with picky or finicky behavior).

A wise woman will not neglect her external appearance, but will spend more time developing a beautiful inner character that is spoken of highly in the Bible.

"Your beauty should not come from outward adornment, such as braided hair and the wearing of gold jewelry and fine clothes. Instead, it should be that of your inner self, the unfading beauty of a gentle and quiet spirit, which is of great worth in God's sight. For this is the way the holy women of the past who put their hope in God used to make themselves beautiful." (1 Peter 3:3-5a, NIV)

How to Attract Anyone Worth Attracting

While all the above is indeed interesting, there really is a key to attracting the opposite sex into a lasting relationship. Many people have discovered it, and often they have very satisfying life-long partnerships. These people realized either consciously or subconsciously that they didn't want to trick people into liking them or start relationships based on false facades. Why would you want another person to like you when you are acting like someone who isn't really you? You certainly don't want someone being attracted to you because of temporary factors like physical beauty which is guaranteed to evanesce in a decade or two. What you need is for the other person to like you for who you are, and for the enduring quality of your personality.

That conclusion naturally leads to the real key. The trick to attracting a quality mate is to first be quality yourself. By "quality" I mean being confident and content in who you are created to be in Christ, and living the Christ-life with integrity and authenticity. You must become a quality person to attract a quality person. Nothing less will do. Nothing more is needed. If you are a "great catch" you'll find many suitors, and hopefully you'll have wisdom to discern which is best for you.

If you work to create maturity and inner beauty, if you strive to be the "right person" for others, you will not fail to be attractive. Furthermore, you will be most attractive to people who have likewise developed inner beauty and so who can recognize it in you. You will be able to attract anyone worth attracting.

As Christians we can take this principle one step further: the key to attracting a life-long mate of exceptional quality is to become more like Christ. Who wouldn't want to marry a person with the characteristics of Jesus? He embodied strength and gentleness, purity and power, compassion and justice. Jesus had passion, plenty of drive, exuded wisdom and possessed maturity far beyond his years. Jesus may not have been much to look at physically, based on Isaiah 53:2 which says "He grew up before him like a tender shoot, and like a root out of dry ground. He had no beauty or majesty to attract us to him, nothing in his appearance that we should desire him." (NIV). Still, there has never been anyone with more inner beauty. It turns out that no matter how old you are it is not too late nor too early to start becoming more like Christ, and allowing God to create within you a maturity and an inner beauty that is beyond this world.

After attraction comes relationship, though of course attraction also is present in relationship. But how do we go from initial attraction to creating deeper relationships? In the next chapter we will discover how relationships mature, how we can grow deeper while guarding our hearts, and we'll briefly discuss the stages relationships often go through on the way toward disintegration.

CHAPTER TWO FURTHER LEARNING

1) Rank order the 5 ways people are attracted to each other, starting with which of the 5 is most important to you.

2) What do you find most attractive about Christ?

3) What must you do to become the person you are looking for is looking for?

4) Which of the topics listed in this chapter can you grow to become more attractive?

5) Do you overemphasize physical beauty, even though you know it is fleeting? Why?

6) On a 1 to 10 scale, how mature are you? How can you grow to be more mature?

7) On a 1 to 10 scale, how much inner beauty do you have? What can you do to foster inner beauty?

CHAPTER 3

Would you give up a rib? How Attraction Develops into Intimacy

"You come to love not by finding the perfect person, but by seeing an imperfect person perfectly." —Sam Keen[14]

As a university professor I attend many weddings, and as an ordained minister I have even officiated some of them. Weddings typically happen when one or both of the partners are graduating, though sometimes people can't wait for graduation to "get hitched." Almost all of these occasions feature happy couples, slightly sad and nostalgic parents, many well-wishers, and often both some deep and some shallow reflections on love. Many times pastors include the little chat about how Eve was not made from Adam's head to rule over him, nor from his feet to be trampled by him, but from his rib to rule creation beside him. We accept this truth, but I think we often miss the fact that Eve didn't come without a price: she cost Adam a rib!

Having cracked a rib playing soccer, I can say Adam was lucky all this took place before the Fall and the advent of pain. My rib hurt for a long time. I wonder if after the Fall Adam felt the pain occasionally then looked at Eve and smiled, thinking that it was so very worth it. Adam lost a rib for Eve; what are you willing to do to find your perfect mate and grow the relationship? Are you willing to be vulnerable and face rejection? Are you mature enough to enter relationships that may terminate with pain? This chapter looks at the price and process of intimacy, looking at Social Penetration Theory, the stages of relationship development and the stages of relationship deterioration.

Social Penetration Theory and Stages of Intimacy Development

While the above five "Attraction Factors" may clarify why we are attracted to someone, they don't help us understand how relationships develop into romances. Social Penetration Theory, first proposed by Irwin Altman and Dalmas Taylor (1973)[15], describes the gradual process that results in relational closeness. They propose that through self-disclosure people move incrementally toward each other, potentially resulting in intimacy.

Self-disclosure means simply revealing something about ourselves, and while this is most often done verbally, it could also be done nonverbally by giving a gift or showing someone a place that is special to you. As we reveal things about ourselves we become vulnerable to the other person's rejection or criticism, and thus it takes true courage to initiate a relationship. To me, this is why God gave men courage—not to face bullets on a battlefield but to face the possibility of initiating a conversation with a woman!

Our cultural norm has men initiating romantic relationships, though this could change as our gender roles shift. It certainly is more acceptable today for women to initiate a relationship than it was in the past, and often guys are more flattered than turned off by a forward woman. However, most likely males will continue to initiate in the majority of relationships because they have a higher degree of risk acceptance (caused by testosterone's effect on the brain) and because they are more attracted by visual stimulation. After years of observation I can't help but wonder, however, if the man really initiates or if the women is actually choosing through her nonverbal communication the guy who will eventually choose her.

Regardless of the cause, women seem to be perfectly made to respond to self-disclosure courage, and they are much better at reciprocating than men. If a woman initiates, the man may not know how to hold a conversation, and often there is an awkward silence. This is much more rare with women, who seem to naturally take their cue to not only accept the initiator but to in turn reciprocate with self-disclosure of their own. As the two people share more and more about themselves and refuse to criticize or reject the other, the relationship deepens.

Typically self-disclosure occurs rapidly at first and

decelerates as the relationship grows. This is because at first we are very curious and want the other person to understand us. Most of the conversation is about good things we have done and includes attempts to make more connections with the other person. As time elapses there are fewer things we feel they **must** know about us, and there are more things that we may hesitate to share because the details may put us in a negative light.

Conversations often start with our "public personae," which are things that are readily apparent. Often more superficial topics help us initiate a conversation. In just about every culture small talk about the weather serves as a connection point, because it is an environment we share with others. In most of the world you can also talk about your job, though in France that is thought to be a deeper level of relationship, so they more quickly bring up their lineage. In any case, often you go from superficial topics like the weather or your job to more personal matters.

As you deepen the level of self-disclosure, you peel back another layer of yourself and subject it to the scrutiny of the other. In my experience we start with superficial "cliché" topics like the weather and then progress to issues of facts, such as what you do for a living or where you are traveling. The facts then deepen and get more personal, such as how many kids are in your family, and this often leads to a discussion of preferences. At this stage you may talk about a book you like or give your impression of a celebrity or explain why you like a certain TV show. This level obviously only can be reached after cliché and facts because there is a real chance that the other person may "reject" some of your preferences. If you trust them and have built a solid relationship to this point, you can accept their disliking some of your preferences in the process of exploring to see if you share other areas of agreement. While the factual level may have some personal information, the preferences level is more personal because there is a stronger link to your emotions which are arguably formed by a fairly stable set of personal characteristics and assumptions.

The preferences stage gives way to the opinion stage, in which you are not only expressing how you feel about something but also explaining how you processed those feelings and what conclusions you have drawn. Here you talk about what you believe to be the case in matters such as politics or relationships.

After the opinion stage you finally reach the level that many relationships never develop beyond, and that is the values stage. In the values stage you may take a controversial position on some matter that is important to you, or you may talk about your religious convictions or even political actions. These more personal topics are quite charged and reveal more about yourself as well as have an even higher propensity to put you at odds with the other person. Indeed, if you find a disagreement at the values level it may create a real fissure in the relationship, and it doesn't take very many disagreements at this level to result in a breakup. No one is going to argue or break-up over the day being rainy, but people could challenge your religious perspective or what you think the answer is to the turmoil in the Middle East. You may be so upset by these kinds of differences that you don't wish to talk to them again.

Many relationships go quickly through the cliché, facts, preferences and opinions stages then stagnate before reaching the values stage. This is because the couples go too fast in the early stages and now are unwilling to go deeper and expose the relationship to threatening topics. Problematically, relationships that do not deepen often only weaken. While a pause between the opinion and values stage may be beneficial, if the relationship doesn't soon get back on the progression track of reciprocation there could be trouble.

GRAPH 1: CONVERSATION LEVELS

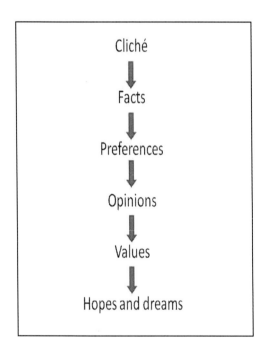

In dating relationships, this is where the lady often discovers that the relationship "isn't going anywhere" and may decide to break up. Paradoxically, the guy may fear going deeper because he doesn't want to hurt the relationship, and he has a stronger need to not expose weakness, so the break up may occur precisely because the guy did not want to risk the relationship.

The final level of relationship intimacy is a person's hopes and dreams and desires. This inner core of personality is mushy and malleable, and not only do we guard it ferociously but we also don't even know it fully ourselves. Sometimes in this center there lingers inner hurt or feelings of worthlessness. Sometimes we don't even know our own innermost longings. To connect on this deepest of levels not only means sharing the most inner thoughts of our hearts but also means exposing those thoughts to the other's influence. Even just sharing them makes us put them into words which means making them more solid and giving them more shape. By sharing these things we also allow the other person to change us first because we shape them to be acceptable to the other and second because we may receive his or her perspective. In this way, whoever shares our innermost core in fact also has a part in shaping that core. If you allow someone to this level of intimacy and then the relationship breaks up, you will be severely affected and often you will have troubles understanding yourself—you'll feel like you lost a part of yourself when they left. Indeed, you may wish it had been a rib that you gave away rather than your heart that the rib was protecting.

While this level can be reached before marriage, it obviously is related to God's declaration that the "two become one flesh." I believe this phrase is essentially describing the physical relationship as we'll discuss in a later chapter, but it certainly also can have a more robust meaning. We connect with our romantic partners on multiple levels, to include physical, intellectual, emotional, and spiritual. While we are constantly bombarded with the Christian message to "save" ourselves for marriage, we often only think of it in a physical context. The Bible, however, wisely admonishes us not only to save sex for marriage but also repeatedly admonishes us to guard our hearts. In many ways this means being careful about whom we allow to reach into our core being.

By now it should be apparent that skipping levels of intimacy or disclosing too fast can result in the other person shutting down because they cannot trust you with their more personal information. Trust is earned over time, and the fear of rejection can be a powerful force in a person's life, especially if he or she has a troubled past. At the same time, failure to move forward can also endanger the relationship. Some other characteristics that should be noted include:

1) Relationships grow deeper due in part to vulnerability on both sides.
2) Self-disclosure should be reciprocal at all levels, especially in the early stages.
3) You need to spend more time at each progressive level until at the core you can spend an entire lifetime discovering and being discovered.

A final facet of the self-disclosure model that is less apparent is the fact that it involves not just revealing information about yourself but also being interested in the other. John Tarrant[16] once said, "Attention is the most basic form of love; through it we bless and are blessed." If they are not interested (attracted by) in you, then no amount of self-disclosure will win them over.

While the above discussion of conversation levels is mostly my own musings, it should be noted that Irwin Altman and Dalmas Taylor speak of five distinct stages as well. First, the "orientation stage" is when we "play it safe" with small talk and follow social norms. Second, in the "exploratory stage" we start to actually reveal ourselves by expressing our attitudes about moderate topics. This stage is when we become casual friends, and many relationships do not go past this stage. Third, in the "affective stage" we start to talk about more private or personal matters, and it is here that the first criticism and arguments often arise. In a romantic situation, the physical relationship often progresses to intimate touching and kissing. The fourth stage called "stable" involves the partners being capable of sharing just about anything and being able to predict each other's responses. Finally, relationships may go through a "depenetration" stage when the relationship starts to break down and people calculate that they would be happier separate than together. During this stage people cease being vulnerable and disclosing, which is a natural prelude to relationship termination.

Reserve Saying "I love you"

As you can see, often the physical relationship correlates to the interpersonal communication stages of development. This correlation is especially strong for women, who are typically more concerned about connecting on a personal level before advancing the physical relationship. While both genders may be physically aroused enough to bypass connecting at a deeper level, this often results in embarrassment and confusion. A stable long-term relationship is best built on a solid interpersonal communication foundation that then naturally progresses to a physical relationship as well.

As Christians, it is important to proceed with caution when developing the physical relationship. God designed male-female physical relationships to be a kind of slippery slope that gains momentum as you progress, and that means it is all too easy to succumb to physical intimacy prematurely. Once you cross a boundary, it seems far too natural to disregard that boundary and start assaulting the next. The trick is to set boundaries and progress slowly, savoring each dimension without being in a rush to get to the next level of physical intimacy. Instead of focusing on the physical, you should focus on building the interpersonal relationship, while realizing there is a connection between the two. Ideally you will time the physical progression so that you do not go "too far" before marriage but instead will enter marriage with both purity and familiarity, prepared to experience true physical intimacy at its best.

We'll discuss more on sexuality in a later chapter, but here we are concerned with setting up boundaries in the communication realm that will also serve to slow down physical intimacy. One of the best ideas is to reserve saying "I love you" until you really mean it. Far too often these three words are thrown out on a first date or used to actually express an emotion of desire so that they really mean "I lust for you." It is far wiser to hold the word "love" in great esteem, and understand that it means far more than just a temporary emotion. Love is the willingness to choose the other's good over your own, the willingness to sacrifice for the other, and the desire to enjoy the other and support them so that they can be all they can be. Indeed, real love would never hurt the other person by going too far, but would protect the other's sexual purity.

My wife decided at 13 that she would reserve saying "I love you" for her future spouse, and I believe this dedication went a long way toward protecting her from inappropriate physical relationships. If you do not say "I love you," you will greatly impede physical intimacy. On the other hand, immature or immoral boys often try to talk a lady into going too far and will pour out their false words of love and devotion. Real love should not need so many words but instead should be developed by actions of respect and sacrifice.

Knapp Relationship Progression Stages

There are many other ways to look at relationship progression that can help you understand where you are in a relationship and where the relationship is most likely going. M. L. Knapp [17] divides relationships into three phases: coming together, relational maintenance, and coming apart. While the first and last phases occur almost automatically, the middle phase is the most enjoyable and requires the most work. No model can perfectly describe every relationship, but Knapp's does a good job of describing the typical stages of relationship formation and disintegration, allowing you to develop an idea of where your relationship is and where it is going.

The first stage of the Coming Together phase is called "initiation," which just means you meet and make your first impressions. Research suggests that most people will form a strong impression of you in the first 7-17 seconds and that 55% of that impression is based on physical appearance[18], so it is beneficial to pay some attention to physical factors (clothing, smell, hair style, etc.). Other first impression characteristics include your communication abilities, ranging from pleasantness of voice to vocabulary, and what can easily be discerned about your character, attitudes, and energy levels. This first stage of relationships only involves light conversation as you begin to assess the possibilities (benefits and detriments) of working toward a personal relationship.

The second stage is called "experimentation," in which two people attempt to find common interests. Typically this stage is characterized by probing questions searching for social connections or rapid speech explaining how you see the world and hoping they see it similarly. Many relationships never go deeper than this stage, which is essentially just friendship.

Beginning the "maintenance" phase is the "intensifying" stage characterized by increasing self-disclosure and reciprocity. Sometimes this is where you will "DTR" (define the relationship), and often you will give gifts and express commitment or affection. During this stage you transition to something more than being "just friends," and you may begin to use "we" language, even about things you think (for example, saying "We don't like black licorice").

Growing through the third stage leads to "integration", which is when the lives of the two people begin to merge, and they think of themselves as a couple. Typically the two people start combining their social circles and get to know each other's friends and family. Often their lives conjoin so that they develop inside humor, gain unspoken understanding of each other, and share intimacy trophies. In our society they may even claim a particular song as "their" song, and often relationships at this stage involve increasing levels of physical intimacy as well as heavy amounts of self-disclosure.

The final stage of relationship development is called "bonding," when a public declaration of commitment is made. Often this is done through marriage, and intimate/romantic relationships can remain here indefinitely (with some effort). Some keys to successfully staying "bonded" are having appropriate power sharing mechanisms, developing positive and constructive communication patterns, and making frequent "friendship" connections with one another instead of allowing the relationship to drift apart.

The first two deterioration stages can also be considered part of the "maintenance" phase. Throughout this phase (in the integrating, bonding, differentiating, and circumscribing stages) couples have to work to continue having a positive relational experience, whereas the lower three stages on this pyramid (see graph 2) come rapidly and almost effortlessly in succession.

In the "differentiating" stage couples cease discovering commonalities and begin to highlight differences. Partners take note of habits in the other person that annoy them, and they become more individualistic in their thinking instead of always considering the world from the perspective of a couple.

GRAPH 2: KNAPP STAGES

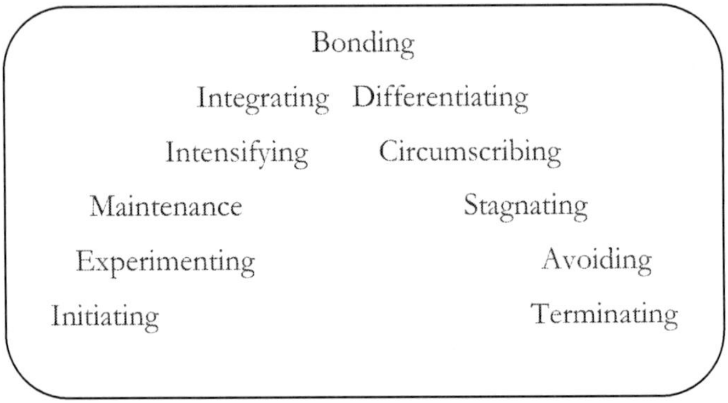

```
               Bonding
      Integrating  Differentiating
        Intensifying    Circumscribing
      Maintenance         Stagnating
      Experimenting          Avoiding
    Initiating               Terminating
```

Stage two is called "circumscribing," when instead of just noticing differences, the couple puts in place boundaries (spoken or implied) to communication. Self-disclosure slows down, and communication becomes much more shallow with a reduced range of topics. Often this is a self-reinforcing cycle, and partners avoid conversations that are controversial. Instead of dealing with issues, they create more swaths of silence. John Gottman', a physiologist who studies divorce, once stated that "relationships end in a whimper" rather than in a burst of outrage. Controversy and even heated conversation and arguments are not as dangerous as silence for a relationship.

If the relationship continues to deteriorate it reaches the

"stagnation" stage, which is part of the "coming apart" phase. From here, a lot of inertia develops that makes it nearly impossible to reverse the decline. At this stage the couple stops most positive interaction and has a general feeling that "nothing changes." Often for dating relationships the woman recognizes that the relationship is "going nowhere" and resolves to end it. Or, in a marriage, the two partners have lived with pain so long that they cannot see how the relationship can improve.

After the despair of stagnation comes the avoidance stage when communication is reduced to bare functional necessity. Partners may actually avoid each other altogether, not wanting each other's company. For marriages this may be a separation stage, whereas for dating relationships this stage may be very short but involve a partner declining to go with the other to an event or failing to meet when they usually do.

The final stage is called "termination" when the couple formally dissolves the relationship. Although it is possible to save a relationship or even "relight the fire" after this stage, typically termination is permanent. While it is always bad if a marriage fails, disintegration of other relationships is not necessarily a bad thing. Also note that all relationships are unique and so move at different speeds and are affected by personalities and particular circumstances.

Courting instead of Dating: Bad habits are hard to break

Christians offer a lot of advice on the subject of dating, and often it is contradictory. The term "courting" is now popular in Christian circles because it is thought to better define the process from a Christian perspective. In truth, the Bible has very little to say on the subject of how men and women relate before marriage, so instead of making sweeping all-inclusive declarations, it is much wiser to offer guidelines and insist that they only be considered with discretion and flexibility.

Many Christians feel dating is inherently wrong, while others can't imagine anything dangerous about the practice. For our purposes, "dating" describes the culturally popular practice of two people of the opposite gender getting together to do a fun activity with the intent of getting to know one another better. Often this leads to "going steady" which is an exclusivist relationship in which the two individuals voluntarily give up their rights to date other people. Courting, in my opinion, is the practice of two people getting to know each other deeply with the intent of discovering if they are compatible for marriage. This functionally looks a lot like dating, though it should emphasize getting to know each other's families more as those families will influence the final decision, and it should focus on long-term compatibility rather than just physical attraction. Courting is not as hedonistic as dating; it is not so much concerned with having immediate pleasure together as it is with understanding ultimate compatibility. Finally, courting clearly means that the relationship should be nurtured and protected, but if one partner knows the other is not his or her life-mate, the courting relationship needs to immediately end. If the relationship has remained honorable and pure, then a Christian friendship can endure, but if too many physical boundaries have been crossed, it becomes nearly impossible to "just be friends."

In my mind, dating is not evil or wrong, but it is fraught with potential pitfalls. The main problem with dating is that it may lead to premature physical intimacy since the two people are basically in the relationship to please themselves, whereas courting progresses slower and more methodically. Dating tends to be an emotional rollercoaster in which the friendship stage is skipped, laying an incomplete foundation that quickly erodes and leads to relationship dissolution. Another serious problem is that when something is not pleasing in a dating relationship, the couple simply breaks up, and this practice repeated may lead to a habit of giving up on relationships when the going gets tough. It also likely leads to having many more romantic-intentioned relationships than does courting, resulting in more temptation. Other objections to dating include that it develops a self-centered, feeling-oriented conception of love, that it may develop an appetite for variety and change which creates dissatisfaction within marriage, and that it often isolates a couple from other vital relationships[19]. In fact, many young women find that after they break up from dating many other relationships are in shambles and they feel alone and without a support structure when they most need it.

Greg Williams, marriage counselor and moderator of the TV show *Marriage Unleashed*, goes so far as to call dating "preparation for divorce." He often talks about how courting is the older and more enduring practice and that in many ways dating was just a cultural step between courting and the current practice of "hooking up" or having "friends with benefits." These practices are anti-Biblical, and result in pain and destruction that often not only harms the current relationship but also subsequent relationships.

Scientific Reasons to Avoid Physical Intimacy Before Marriage

Some may think avoiding premature physical intimacy is only justified by religious reasoning, but science has discovered strong biochemical reasons to limit ones number of paramours. Dating produces an amphetamine-like rush of dopamine, nor-epinephrine and phenylethylaminein in the brain, but over time the body builds up a tolerance to these chemicals. It seems reasonable that God intended the initial chemical rush to help "jump-start" more permanent bonds between life-partners. If these rushes are frequently repeated, they lose their power, and people start a dangerous loop of looking for an emotional high while not realizing each high makes the next one harder to get. The more you date, and the more intimate your physical contact, the more physical stimulation you'll need to get the same emotional high, and so obviously it can very easily lead to sexual activity as you seek the level of arousal that you felt before.

Multiple sexual relationships are especially to be avoided, not just because all extra-marital sex is sin but also because two people having sex releases oxytocin and the vasopressin hormone (in men), which create a biochemical bond between partners. God intended this bond to assist couples to stay together for life. According to researchers at the University of California, oxytocin has been shown to be "associated with the ability to maintain healthy interpersonal relationships and healthy psychological boundaries with other people."[20] It is released from the pituitary gland in increasing amounts corresponding to increasing amounts of physical intimacy, ranging from small amounts when holding hands to large doses being released during sexual orgasm. The more physical contact (and especially sex) a couple shares, the greater the chemical-emotional bond and the more painful relationship dissolution and forming new relationships will be.

Furthermore, endorphins (the body's natural pain killers) also play a key role in long-term relationships and are released during intimate moments including sexual activity. Endorphins create a general sense of well-being and security, and are considered addictive, which may explain why so many young people who have once experimented with sex get hooked and trapped into increasingly unhealthy relationships. When the first phase of sexual intimacy passes, it is the endorphin-enhanced sense of peace and well-being that endures and encourages couples to stay together for life. Interrupting this natural process of bonding by continuous forming and breaking decreases not only the likeliness but also the biochemical rewards of long-term relationships.

It seems much wiser to have all these chemicals and hormones working for a marriage instead of expending them on a series of sexual flings leading to difficulties bonding with a future life mate. Studies show that people who have many sexual partners struggle to connect on a deeper level, have a hard time committing to marriage, and have a higher frequency of divorces if they do marry. Our bodies seem to have been designed for heterosexual monogamous relationships, with chemicals being set in place to move relationships toward sexual intimacy, keeping couples together by a shared brain-chemical bond and naturally transitioning from adrenaline-pumped physical attraction toward long-term intimacy and stability in which the partners feel comfort and satisfaction in each others' presence.

I feel the ideal is to court instead of date, since all indicators suggest having fewer serious suitors before marriage is advisable. In a way, courting is pretty much just dating with a purpose and at a slower pace. The key is to understand what you are doing instead of getting swept away by the process and to intentionally put in place boundaries that help slow down the process. These boundaries will be discussed more in Chapter 5.

For me, the first step is not going out one-on-one but carefully evaluating a potential mate on group dates or at group functions. Church youth or college group activities are perfect for observing others, getting to know their character, and assessing their compatibility. That's how I met my wife. I was teaching a college group Bible study one night, and when Rebecca walked through the door I felt God saying, "There's the one for you." My reply was less than romantic, as I thanked God for the revelation but asked Him to help me not allow her to distract me from teaching. For the next few weeks I ensured Rebecca was invited to all our church functions so I could get to know her better. At one point she noticed I always sat beside her and struck up conversations, so she asked a friend if I was interested in her. The friend replied that I was "just being nice" so that she would feel comfortable in the church and that

I acted that way with everyone.

I should probably hasten to add, in case it sounds like an abuse of my position, that Rebecca is the same age as I am. I also asked the church leadership if they were okay with our dating to ensure there was no undue influence due to my teaching status. In any case, I got to know her in a public setting, and only after I had ensured there were no obvious reasons we shouldn't be together did I initiate activities for just us two.

Rebecca (now my wife) and I have had many discussions on the subject of dating because we had very different experiences. She had many dates that typically remained rather superficial, whereas I married the second person I solo "dated" (I would call my behavior courting). Despite our differences, in the end both patterns worked for us because we both were very careful to guard our hearts and not get too serious too soon. We also both strove to get to know the other person as a friend first, and we did not get too physically-involved until we had observed the other person in many situations and carefully considered the relationship. I feel courting is a better pattern to meet these objectives, but I admit they can also be met by a person who dates.

Whether or not you court instead of dating, you are wise to proceed at a slow pace. According to Ted Huston at the University of Texas, the speed at which courtship progresses often determines the ultimate success of a relationship. His research found that the longer the courtship, the stronger the long-term relationship. From a purely biochemical standpoint, this makes sense since feelings of passionate love lose strength over time. After two or three years the chemicals responsible for passionate love (adrenaline, dopamine, nor epinephrine, phenyl ethylamine, etc.) dwindle significantly. Suddenly you may notice your lover's faults and may even wonder why they changed. Most likely your partner didn't change, but you now see them more rationally without the blinding hormones of infatuation. At this point your relationship is either built on more than physical attraction and strong enough to endure, or it goes through serious turmoil. If the relationship is solid, it can advance and receive other chemical boosts as the endorphins continue to provide a sense of well-being and security, and the hormones oxytocin and vasopressin that produce feelings of satisfaction and attachment are released during physical contact.

In summary, it is wise to be very selective when finding a romantic partner, and you should try to develop your romantic relationship slowly. Setting clear boundaries and delaying most physical intimacy until marriage is the best option, and deciding to court instead of date may assist you in accomplishing that goal. Be sure to get to know the other person as a friend during group functions, and only after laying some solid groundwork through self-disclosure and discovering similarities in the intensifying stage are you ready to advance to the maintenance phase when you must continually invest in the relationship to keep it healthy. If you try to substitute physical contact for personal connection, you not only are hurting your current relationship but also you may be damaging the future relationship you want to last a lifetime.

Hopefully this chapter has made it clear that building

relationships is no easy task. Not only does it take courage to self-disclose, and dedication to move through Knapp's stages but also our biochemistry can make resisting sexual temptation simultaneously important and difficult. People have to ask themselves how important a relationship is and if they are willing to "give up a rib" to invest in building a relationship that will last a lifetime. In the next chapter we will look at love, explore how to be better at it, and hopefully look at how to know when we are in it.

CHAPTER THREE FURTHER LEARNING

1) Do you have different definitions to distinguish dating and courting? Do you think one of these is wrong?

2) How good are you at self-disclosure? How could you get better at it?

3) Which stages of Knapp's relationship model have you been through?

4) How malleable is your core personae (hopes, dreams, aspirations, etc.)?

5) As you age your core becomes more hardened. How does this affect self-disclosure for older couples?

6) Have you ever self-disclosed to God, sharing your deepest intimacies with Him, and letting Him help form them?

CHAPTER 4

It was Good: What's Love and Is There Just One Right One For Me?

"When you are in love you can't fall asleep because reality is finally better than your dreams." —Dr. Seuss[21]

Have you ever been in love? How did you know? It's so easy to confuse infatuation with real love or to allow our emotions and desires to get the best of us in the heat of the moment then regret it later. Far too often people are blinded by physical attraction and declare unending love for someone only later to see another side of their lover and regret the relationship. We often are confused by love and do not even know our own hearts. I remember as a young teenager being absorbed in wondering if someone "liked" me only to eventually discover they did but that I didn't really "like" them in that way at all. It would have been so much better to first have known my own heart. This chapter will hopefully help our heads understand our hearts so that we can better interpret the familiar twinge of excitement that tells us romance is in the air. We will explore what love is and if there is only one Mr. or Mrs. Right for us.

My own experience with love at an early age was fairly limited. I remember in kindergarten I refused to play boy-chase-girl but hypocritically engaged in girl-chase-boy nearly every recess. In grade school and middle school I occasionally had girls trying to be my "secret admirer," but for the most part I knew who they were and just tried not to pay them much attention while being careful to let them down easily to avoid embarrassing them. When I was eleven-years old we moved to Denmark and I was assigned a fourteen-year-old translator who also happened to be the prettiest young lady in the school. She developed a crush on me, probably because I was so exotic (being from America), and while I liked her I wasn't ready for a relationship. One Friday afternoon after gym class I got a love letter from her asking me to check a box saying either "I love you" or "I do not love you" and admonishing me that the worst thing I could do was not reply. I remember being haunted all weekend by it, too embarrassed to tell my parents, and then being so flustered by the conundrum that I never replied. The young lady was understandably never as friendly toward me again.

Back in America for high school, all of a sudden the boy-girl attraction greatly increased. Instead of ignoring ladies to play soccer, I played soccer hoping the ladies would notice my skills. Still, other than having a crush at a Christian camp, and going on some double dates mostly to school dances, I only seriously dated two women in my life. I thought I was in love with the first lady, but I know I was with the second. The first relationship was with an outstanding young lady I met at church, and it lasted five years. The second relationship is happily still continuing, and will do so "till death do us part." I could have married the first girl I dated, but it would have been the wrong choice for me. I am so glad I listened to God and found a person He intended for me.

Had I not broken up with the first lady, I would have missed the right one for me. This should give people strong motivation to limit dating so that they are available when the right one comes along. In my case with the first girlfriend, we were not just dating (learning more about a person by doing things together), but we were seriously courting (getting to know a person and their family for the purpose of deciding if we should marry). We had a great relationship, I liked her family, and she felt God wanted us to marry. I told her as soon as God confirmed His will to me we'd get engaged.

It just never happened. Our relationship had some passion, and also was a great friendship, with some people describing it more as if we were siblings than courting. We never argued or had a single dispute that I can remember. To be fair, two of the years were spent as a long distance relationship because I went to college, but even that can't very well justify the long duration only to terminate the relationship. I liked her, and I wanted her to be the right one. But she wasn't.

After five years of courting I finally realized that I had

been earnestly praying God would confirm the relationship and hadn't listened to His overwhelming silence to that prayer. As soon as I got serious and asked Him if I should break up with her, I felt God confirming that decision. Before then I had never really submitted to the possibility that it wasn't in God's will for my life but only wanted His confirmation of my will. When it became obvious to me that God had a different plan, we had a peaceful yet somewhat tearful breakup followed by a few platonic letters before we allowed time to sweep us into new things. In fact, she ran into a childhood sweetheart and was married within the year, and I met Rebecca only eight months after the breakup and married her just over a year after we met.

As it happened in my case, often the exact wrong mate comes just before the exact right one. This is a good person whom you think would make a good spouse, but as business guru Jim Collins says, "Good is the enemy of Great" because you settle for it. I have seen time and time again couples thinking they had the right person to marry only to eventually discover incompatibilities or realize their own hearts were saying "no" even as their heads were arranging the engagement. Often part of the problem is that the couple has gone too far physically, creating a bond that shouldn't exist (we'll discuss that more later). Sometimes, as in my case, there simply is no reason to break up, but that isn't sufficient reason to go ahead and marry. So watch out for the exact wrong one. Many young men have thanked me for this advice when they quickly found their life mate after a difficult breakup, though few of them were enthusiastic at the prospect of ending a good relationship in which they had significant investment.

We must strive to do all we can to ensure we marry the right person and have God's blessing on our relationships. Satan would like few things more than to get two people married for the wrong reasons. His plan to destroy marriage starts before the wedding, as he knows that a solid Christian union is a powerful testimony to God's grace and an active reminder of what true love looks like. Our building of a solid marriage also starts well before we meet our future spouse. In a way, it actually starts when we first begin to learn how to love.

What's Love?

This question has plagued most of us at some point, and it has haunted many poets attempting to at least describe the intense feelings of affection and passion that overcame them. Most of us would interpret it as love if we felt a sort of drifting moodiness in thought and behavior, a narrowing of vision such that the entire universe revolved around one other person, and a conviction that no one else has ever felt so smitten. But then again, love doesn't always feel like that. Love has been described as ecstasy and torment, freedom and slavery, the creator of war and of peace, and some would say it is what "makes the world go 'round." While the earth's motion is probably not impacted, sales of books, movies, and songs would certainly topple if they could not be about the topic of love (or at least its cousin lust).

Since poets and entertainers cannot adequately define love, scientists took a stab at it. Unlike anger and fear, love turned out to be intensely difficult to quantify. A raised heart rate or extra sweat hardly indicates love every time, and how could you be sure love is absent even when there are no physical indicators? Some researchers tried to reduce love to just the sexual act since that is obviously needed for genetic reproduction and can be studied. Various anthropologists went so far as to dismiss love entirely, saying that it is irrelevant and only amounts to a culturally-conditioned phenomena. In their minds, love is just a label—peasants have sex whereas aristocrats (and moderns) have time to call it "falling in love."

Contrary to these opinions put forth by people who apparently have more brain than heart, we now have conclusive scientific evidence that love is trans-cultural and not simply a product of cultural-conditioning. How it is expressed, whether it is related to marriage, and a myriad of other aspects of love are certainly products of culture, but anthropologists William Jankowiak of the University of Nevada-Las Vegas and Edward Fischer of Tulane University found evidence of romantic love in 147 of the 166 cultures they studied. Jankowiak wrote that love "... is, instead, a universal phenomenon, a panhuman characteristic that stretches across cultures. Societies like ours have the resources to show love through candy and flowers, but that does not mean that the lack of resources in other cultures indicates the absence of love."[22]

In many ways love is beyond description or quantification. Philosophers would tell us that love is a Platonic Form like Beauty or Goodness, transcendent of space and time. These concepts describe fundamental reality, or the true essence of creation; they are so simple that we all apprehend what is meant immediately, but they are also so complex that no one can comprehend them or perfectly describe them.

While poets, scientists, and even philosophers seem rather out of their league when it comes to defining love satisfactorily, there is a good chance that we can get a more satisfying answer from theologians. In Christianity we have a God who embodies love, as the Bible goes so far as to say "God is love" (1 John 4:8, NIV). Unfortunately, there are too few people who have actually read the Bible sufficiently to get a full picture of who God is or what His kind of love entails. Most people like the love of the New Testament that deals with always forgiving sins or treating others as we want to be treated, but they seldom graduate to understand the strong love of God's character that prompted Him to die for humanity but also allows Him to be willing to lose His beloved creations to the flames of Hell if they refuse His lordship.

The best description of love given to humanity is Paul's exposition in 1 Corinthians 13. In this chapter Paul extols the preeminence of love, then proceeds to define love by saying:

"Love is patient, love is kind. It does not envy, it does not boast, it is not proud. 5 It is not rude, it is not self-seeking, it is not easily angered, it keeps no record of wrongs. 6 Love does not delight in evil but rejoices with the truth. 7 It always protects, always trusts, always hopes, always perseveres. 8 Love never fails." (1 Corinthians 13:1, NIV).

Paul then continues to suggest love is eternal and perfect

and that expressing it constitutes true maturity. Perhaps the most accurate (but still incomplete) way to boil down the definition is to say love is the opposite of selfishness. In many ways love is caring for others above self and therefore being willing to sacrifice yourself for another. Jesus said, "Greater love has no one than this, that he lay down his life for his friends" (John 15:13, NIV). That definition found its fullest expression in the person of Jesus Christ who literally laid down His life for us on the cross so that He could pay the price of our sin, satisfy justice and redeem us to receive God's mercy. Jesus gave up His rightful place in Heaven to take the form of humanity and was willing to suffer a criminal's death on a cross out of love for His bride (see Phil. 2:1-11).

Perhaps the best simple definition of love is self-sacrifice, and that is why it is so often misunderstood. It can feel great while simultaneously hurting. It could even be understood as being willing to hurt for another. For some people it is impossible to love because they are too in love with themselves to put someone else first. These people still seek romantic relationships, but theirs is a parody of love. They want to be in a love relationship because it makes them feel good, not because it is good for the other person. To truly be in love is not to just be in love with love (i.e., how you feel when you are in love) but to honestly decide that you will sacrifice yourself for another. If you are willing to give up your material possessions — your hopes and dreams, your aspirations and all that you are for the sake of another person, then you probably are in love.

And here lies the crux of the issue. ***Love is not a feeling*** *at all, though feelings often accompany it. Love is a choice. It is a continuously refreshed decision to be committed to another person.* The reason God can command us to love is because loving is an act of the will, not the emotions. God Himself was not compelled by emotion to die for us, but rather God is love, so He acted out His identity to become our Savior and ultimately our eternal Father. He acted sacrificially, giving of Himself absolutely, so that we may have an intimate relationship with Him forever.

The Bible can be seen as one great love story about a God who pursues humanity, as opposed to all other religions in which humanity pursues God. God had a perfect relationship with Adam and Eve in the Garden of Eden until sin intruded. Since God's holy nature prevents His coexistence with sin, God had to deal with this intruder in order to have a close relationship with humanity. At Mount Sinai God gave Moses two important things. First, the Ten Commandments were given so that people would refrain from sin and recognize it in themselves, and second the tabernacle and sacrificial system were given so that sin could be dealt with. God wanted to tabernacle with His people and made a way through sacrifice to remove the stain of sin. Eventually God even allowed Solomon to build a more permanent dwelling for Him on earth, and His glory descended upon and lived in Zion's Temple.

This whole system looked forward to when Jesus would come to be the final sacrifice for sin so God no longer had to be separated from humanity by walls or the temple's great curtain that kept humans outside the Holy of Holies. God sent His Spirit to dwell in our hearts, transforming us at the core of our beings to become what He intends us to be. The Bible's final book, the Revelation of John, is not just about judgment but is primarily about the final wedding of the Bride (Church) to the groom (Christ). Indeed, what is truly "revealed" is the nature of Jesus Christ and the depth of His love for His Church. From cover to cover the Bible is about our relationship to God and His choice to love us and what that has entailed. God's decision to love us has certainly been a tale of sacrifice, and our love for others is also a dedication to be self-giving.

Look again at how Paul describes love. Paul doesn't see "love" as a passive noun but says one who loves is full of selfless action. We do not just "fall in love" but we decide to give love regardless of the circumstances. The power of love is not in its overwhelming emotion but lies in our will properly empowered by God as we imitate His character of steadfast love. Romans 5:5 talks about how "the love of God has been poured out within our hearts through the Holy Spirit" (NIV), which is why we can give love even as God gives it to us.

The primary Hebrew word used for God's love in the Old Testament is *khesed*, which suggests "faithful loving-kindness." It means God has deliberately decided to have affection for us and show kindness to us, and that it emanates not from emotion but from God's choice and His loyalty to us because of that choice. *Khesed* is often described as "unfailing" and "endures forever." This is the covenant/commitment kind of love that we imitate in marriage, as we pledge to love "'til death do us part" regardless of the circumstances. From that pledge onward we continually act out our previously declared and committed love.

The end of love is also our fault rather than the result of some uncontrollable emotion. There can be no "falling out of love" because we never fell into it. Just as we chose to love, it's also a choice to no longer love, and no longer be committed to another person. While that choice may come about gradually as successive small choices, it is still ultimately a choice and not a loss of emotions. This is very encouraging because it means love is not based on the fickle and deceitful heart but on an act of will and decision. Often we cannot even know our own hearts and have to ask God to help search our hearts for us, whereas our will can be known because we direct it.

Unlike English, Hebrew and Greek both have many more shades of the word "love" that are less relevant to a romantic/covenant relationship but still may be useful to understand for less intimate relationships. In the Old Testament *ahab* speaks of a spontaneous, impulsive love, while *raham* suggests compassion or brotherly love. In Greek *eros* (where English gets the words "erotic") describes the sensual/sexual/impulsive love, and *philia* (where English gets words like philosophy and Philadelphia) usually means the sincere and reciprocated love for friend, spouse, or children. All of these types of love are more influenced by emotions but still have at their core the will to choose them or at least the will to give in to the emotions.

Interestingly, the New Testament uses one word for love over 250 times that is seldom found in secular writings. In many ways the New Testament coins the term and injects it with its own desired meaning. *Agape* is used much like *khesed* to describe God's unconditional love for us (John 3:16), how we are to love Him back (Matt. 22:36-40), and how we are to love one another (John 13:34). We are even to love ourselves with agape as we are being re-created into the image of Christ and love our enemies with *agape* regardless of our emotions toward them (Mat 5:44).

Looking at its use in the Bible, we see that *agape* is absolute (cannot be partially or half-heartedly offered), is given freely, cannot be compelled, and is one of the most accurate descriptions of God's nature. *Agape* is not based on self-need or want, is not conditioned on reciprocity or calculation of repayment, and has no regards for the "lovability" of the recipient. To *agape* means to desire the other to have everything you have and more, to be beyond any covetousness or condemnation, to not be possessive except in protection. It drives out fear, seeks the highest good for the other with no thought of benefit to oneself, and often involves self-denial, self-renunciation, personal sacrifice, and great humility. Love is willing to suffer slights, hurts, and abuse for the loved one. Love strives to build others up, nurturing and edifying, and when wounded it doesn't retaliate. In short, *agape* love is committed to give 100% and expect 0% in return.

With this understanding it is easy to see why "love never fails" (I Cor 13:8). Don't we all desire this type of love? If so, then we must start being the kind of persons who can give this type of love. The whole creation was created for this type of love rather than for our current self-seeking definition. If everyone were busy giving love no one would miss out. Sadly, our society has everyone trying to take love and ends up with many hurting and lonely people.

The Biblical *khesed* and *agape* kind of love flies in the face of contemporary romance stories where people often scorn the pledge to love "'til death do us part" in order to realize fleeting "true love" emotions with someone else. The world sees love as an emotion we fall into, and as soon as that emotion fades we fall back out of it, creating a pattern of unstable, painful relationships. If this were true love then we all would be better off avoiding it.

You may think the Christian understanding of love also looks undesirable or unreasonable. Indeed, it seems silly to want to love if love means self-sacrifice. Why love if it means putting yourself as a lower priority than someone else? No one should ever desire to "be in love" since that actually means wanting NOT to get your way but to submit to another. If love is self-sacrifice then a wise person would never seek it.

That may be a fair assessment, but a wiser person will understand that the suffering of self-sacrifice by loving is in fact a purifying suffering that eventually results in our own good. It truly is more blessed to give than receive, and the person who invests heavily in love reaps heavily from love. **Love given away is an investment in the self, as it opens us up to be changed by the other and to receive more of God's love that transforms us into His image.** Giving away love results in our receiving love more. The Bible declares, "He who loves his own wife loves himself" (Ephesians 5:28, NAS). Love is the only force in the universe that when given away, multiples, and when reflected, gains power.

While love is worth giving even without it being returned,

it is of course even better to have love reciprocated in a loving marriage. "Love is everything it's cracked up to be," writes relationship guru Erica Jong. "That's why people are so cynical about it...It really is worth fighting for, risking everything for. And the trouble is, if you don't risk everything, you risk even more."[23] Some readers may feel unwilling to seek a loving relationship, perhaps because of past pain or because they are not mature enough to give real love but are honest enough not to offer false love. Such a decision may be eminently prudent for the short term, as sometimes we need to heal or mature before courting. However, if you don't feel called to be single, then the purpose of "time off" is indeed to be healed or to mature and should result in your being whole enough to love again. Typically the best balm is to snuggle closer to God, to be taught by His spirit, and to practice spiritual disciplines that have the power even to help you control your desires.

To not seek a relationship because you are afraid of getting hurt is like avoiding investing a dollar when the payoff could be a thousand dollars. It may be prudent to wait for a good chance of success, but to never invest would be to never receive the payoff. Even if you lost a few dollars at the beginning, your final result will easily make you forget about the initial pain. While we should guard our hearts and be selective, love reciprocated is worth more than all the pain of failed attempts. It truly is "better to love and have lost than to never have loved at all."

I have mentioned before that a lifelong love is a testament to God's love for us, but I believe marriage is even more than that. Reciprocated love in an intimate relationship on earth is a taste of eternity, where all our relationships will be characterized by self-giving love. Marriage is also a training ground for us to learn how to love even while still on earth. And that love should not only stay in the marriage. I am convinced that loving my wife helps me love others better and that God wants us to eventually love everyone like we love our spouses, with a self-sacrifice that is beyond this world, and that can only be made possible because the living God who embodies love lives within us.

Marriage is a powerful symbol throughout the Bible, and especially bookending its contents. In Genesis 1:27 we see it is part of how we understand the Trinity, as "male and female He created them in His image", and the sexual act expands this symbol to show opposites simultaneously coexisting, as sex is both transcendence and intimacy, both becoming fully ones' self and truly merging with another (Gen 2:24). At the Bible's conclusion marriage becomes the chosen metaphor for Christ's love of His people, as He will return for His glorious bride, and they will be united in love forever.

Is there Just One "Right One" for Me?

You may be thinking "this marriage relationship sounds wonderful and should be discussed more in another book, but right now I want to know how to find the right one for me." I'm often asked during relationship seminars, "Is there just one right person made for me to marry that I have to find?" I like the question because it shows a desire to know God's will and for His will to be enacted in our lives, but I don't like the typical motivation of the question, which is a fear of missing the right person. At its core, this fear is a misunderstanding of the nature of God.

To be honest, we are not told in scripture whether or not there is just one "right one" for us, so any musings on the question must be speculative. What I can say with certainty is that if God planned out a single individual for each of us to marry, He is big enough to put in place the factors that would have us meet, and He loves us enough to give us ample chance to fall in love and marry the intended individual.

Personally, I do not think God has just one person in mind for each of us to marry. He may have two or three...but that is about it. There are clearly many more incorrect choices than correct ones. When I was single, I remember thinking about the probability of meeting someone to marry and thinking it was rather unlikely. That is one of the reasons I asked God to arrange my marriage. I think the real key to finding the best person to marry is to stick close to God and listen to His voice. Instead of spending your time trying to meet others (dating), spend your time getting to know God and doing His work on earth, trusting that He will "supply all of your needs according to His riches in glory"(Phil 4:19, KJV). I have seen time and time again that people who are "looking" can't find, but people who are not "looking" run into the love of their lives.

Let's play out a few numbers here. Say you're a guy, and you are at least moderately physically attracted to about 1 in 20 women that you meet. Of those, many are already married or are too old/young for marriage, reducing the probability of meeting both an attractive and eligible woman to 1 in 50. Let's say that of the 1 in 50, only about every other one is also in any way physically attracted to you, making your odds now at 1 in 100, and all we have dealt with is physical attraction. You'd also need to factor in the other attraction variables (proximity, similarity, complementarity, reinforcement), as well as religious faith, compatible personalities, etc. In the end I think the chances of you meeting one "right" person are well beyond 1 in 1000. How many women do you meet in a year? It could easily take 5 years to meet 1000 women, and you might mess up and meet one of these "eligibles" under poor circumstances, letting that one "get away." By this logic it seems nearly impossible to find the person of your dreams in a reasonable amount of time, so we had better be thankful that God can do the impossible.

Since I realized the odds were stacked against me for finding my future bride, I thought it was very reasonable to simply trust God with the issue. The problem is that God often seems to want me to make decisions for myself. Once I have surrendered the issue to Him, He gives it back to me and lets me find my own path. In this way He matures me, as I strive to know Him, submit to Him, and then make good choices like He would.

In my mind, God doesn't predetermine a single person to be our spouse then make us search for them and hope we don't miss them because this would often result in disaster not only for us but also for the other. What if we weren't listening to God at the key time when the other entered our lives, or what if they weren't listening and were instead dating someone else? Our future would be greatly marred by another's disobedience. Instead, I think there are a number of near "perfect" mates, and no absolutely "perfect" ones. We make the "perfection" in our marriages by loving God first and foremost and allowing Him to love the other through us, and this must happen continuously and is not a consequence of simply picking the right mate.

The most important thing is that we submit the decision to His will. God grants us choice so that we may love Him by giving it back to Him and choosing His will, which is ultimately for our benefit as well. If God didn't give us choice there would be no love but only compulsion. I believe God wants to form our hearts, not force our wills, so He grants us true choice. To say this is also to say He relinquishes choice as He allows me to choose instead of Him determining all things. God doesn't behave this way because He likes giving away choice but because He values love, and without real choice there cannot be real love. A corollary to this is the fact that evil is not created by God, but is a product of our using what was meant for good (the power of choice) incorrectly. In the case of marriage, "evil" means us deciding who we wanted to marry apart from seeking His will on the subject, and it leads to reaping a troubled marriage.

As long as we have submitted the issue of marriage to His will, and we are seriously dedicated to doing that will as it is revealed to us, we often are allowed to make our own choices. Just like I want my son to make choices for himself but I retain the right to make corrections or intervene if there is danger, so God allows us to make choices but will actively intervene if we respect Him and allow Him to do so. When it comes to seeking a lifelong partner, if you do not hear God's voice telling you what to do, you are free to do what you think is right. If you have submitted the issue to God, and ensured sin is not getting between you and hearing His voice, then you can be comfortable not hearing His direct will—He is letting you make choices. God's children never need to be afraid of His silence because what it really means is that He is allowing us to choose.

I think this is true for most decisions, including the decision of who to marry. There is typically more than one "right" choice for us, and God wants us to choose one of the good options. There certainly are many "wrong" choices, and I believe if we submit ourselves to God's will, He will protect us from those. God is also good at redemption, so He can even redeem a poor initial choice of whom to marry by transforming it into a good marriage.

Just a few hundred years ago nearly every culture on earth was practicing marriage by arrangement rather than personal choice, and people back then seem to have had a far lower divorce rate. While I admit there were many other factors at play, and many of their relationships were also dysfunctional but didn't end in divorce due to social pressures, many of their relationships were very successful because they understood love to be a choice rather than an emotion.

Please understand that even though God grants us choice to select a mate, He is still in control, knowing the end and the beginning and able to intervene at any moment. I see God as being big enough to "sovereignly" decide to give up sovereignty so that I may learn to love, yet retaining all intervention power to affect the outcome of my choices as He wishes. What is truly marvelous to consider is that God values love so much that He thinks it is worth paying the price of having free will and all its commensurate potential for evil.

In the next chapter we will look at how we can better understand our own hearts and recognize we are in love. Furthermore, I'll try to tackle the ubiquitous "how far is too far sexually" question and offer some wisdom on how to handle sexual temptation.

CHAPTER FOUR FURTHER LEARNING

1) What is your best (succinct) definition of love?

2) Do you think there is only one "right" one for you?

3) Do you agree that any two good Christians could make a good marriage?

4) What is the most loving relationship you have ever observed? What did you see?

5) Are there other verses in the Bible that you know about that help us understand love?

6) Are you mature enough to be able to give *agape*?

CHAPTER 5

Tree of Knowledge: How Do I Know I'm in Love and How Far is too Far?

"If you kiss on the first date and it's not right, then there will be no second date. Sometimes it's better to hold out and not kiss for a long time. I am a strong believer in kissing being very intimate, and the minute you kiss, the floodgates open for everything else." —Actress Jennifer Lopez[24]

In the Garden of Eden there was very little temptation. Adam and Eve must have wandered endlessly through its lavish foliage marveling at God's creation. There were no insects bugging them, no thorns to avoid, and no predators to fear. Shelter seems to have been unnecessary (since things were watered by mists instead of rain), and food was just an outstretched arm away. Of the billions of trees and plants surrounding them, only the fruit of the tree of the knowledge of good and evil was deemed off limits. Surrounded by inviting creation, the ability to sin was greatly dwarfed by the ability to revel in God's goodness and creation.

Despite the astronomical ratio of good to evil opportunity, Adam and Eve managed to find the one forbidden thing and engage in it. Sadly, in today's world the ratio is reversed, and we persist in following our ancestors' footsteps by seeking to do wrong despite the vast array of other options. We are constantly presented with temptation and sin and find it difficult to spare time to simply enjoy what God created. One survey of retirees asked what they would do differently with their time if they could live again, and one of the most frequent answers was "enjoy more sunrises and sunsets". It seems easy to give in to ubiquitous temptation or to forget God amidst convenient dissipations such as Facebook, television, video games, and iPhones. However, it is nearly impossible not to see God when surrounded by starry nights, deep blue skies, or the lush smells and sights of a verdant forest.

Often we need to avoid the distractions in our world to better know our hearts and to better hear from God. I have found that there is no way to turn God's "volume" up, but I can turn down the "volume" of my life so I can hear Him better. This chapter is about knowing our own hearts, which I believe is indelibly linked to communicating with God. It is especially important to ask God to search our hearts and help us discern them when we are making life-changing decisions (see Psalm 139:23).

Fast, Pray, and Meditate for a Day

The most important decision we face, other than daily surrendering to God's Lordship of our lives, is the decision of who to marry. This decision is actually preceded by "do I court this person?" and "do I love this person?" While there is no way to answer the question "How do I know I'm in love?" to everyone's satisfaction, and the answer may be different for each person, there are some general principles we can apply to assist us in our quest to know our own hearts. The most important thing to recognize is that we must seek God's guidance and not rely on our fickle emotions.

Since we know love is a choice rather than an emotion, it may seem that the answer to this question is easy: We know we are in love when we choose to be in love. This answer is basically true but not entirely instructive nor fully satisfactory without elaboration. Furthermore, it probably gets more accurate the longer one is in a relationship. At the start of a relationship there are so many chemicals and hormones at work that we often are overwhelmed and ready to choose self-sacrificial intimate love without counting the cost and realizing what we're doing. The emotions compel the decision. As a relationship progresses, the cost of love becomes more obvious, the hormones less compulsive, and the need to chose love despite emotions becomes more apparent. Unfortunately, most of us must decide if we are in love while still afflicted by the emotional highs of being in a new relationship. Fortunately, God is not thus afflicted, and can often guide us to knowing our own hearts and understanding His will for our lives.

To deal with any large decision, I advocate that you fast,

pray, and meditate for a whole day. Yes, by "fasting" I mean you go without food and only drink water[25]. You can do this for any amount of time you wish, skipping one meal or more. I suggest one day, three days or seven days. In my experience, by about day 4 you stop being very hungry, and I find it then easier to discern God's voice since I'm not distracted by my body's cravings.

For some reason modern Christians seem to think they can have all the benefits of a deep relationship with God while not investing in that relationship. Many young Christians forsake the spiritual disciplines that have been practiced for 2000 years. Jesus doesn't tell His disciples they must fast. He simply assumes they will, saying "When you fast..." (Mat 6:16, NIV). If there is no more important decision than deciding who you will date/court/marry, you would be silly to neglect fasting about it.

When I fast I spend the time I'd normally eat in prayer and try to pray more often throughout the day as well. I allow the hunger to remind me to pray. Prayer is simply talking to God, and is best done out loud and standing just as we see it exemplified in the Bible. While silent prayer is fine, there is no Biblical precedent for it, and standing will help those sleep-deprived among us who have trouble staying awake and focusing on God. Praying out loud also focuses us and makes the experience more conversational and sincere. Since our brains process about 20% faster than our mouths, we normally can talk and think at the same time, allowing us to hold an intelligent conversation. When we pray silently, however, our brain speed and communication speed are the same, preventing us from going much beyond our initial (pre-planned) subject. Far too many people try to pray silently but then drift off into distraction or even sleep.

Prayer must be made a priority when attempting to discern God's will for your life, and you should not just do all the talking but occasionally stop and listen for the Spirit's voice. Some of my best conversations with God happen in the car, when I turn off the music, put a Bible in the passenger seat, and just start talking. I think the natural quiet moments (because I have to concentrate more on driving) make the conversation more two-way, as I'm forced to allow God time to speak back to me without being impatient at silence.

When you pray for this important decision, treat God like the Heavenly Father He is—tell Him what you like about the other person, how they make you feel, why they might be the right one, what hesitations you have, what factors you do not yet know, and all the other things you'd share with a loving parent. Be sure to also ask Him to search your heart and reveal it to you in the conversation. It is also wise to recruit others to pray for you, asking God to give you wisdom and insight for the courting relationship.

Finally, I like to combine fasting and praying with meditation. While Eastern religions see meditation as clearing the mind, Christian meditation is filling the mind with God's word. The Hebrew word for "meditation" actually translates "muttering" and speaks of their practice of memorizing God's word by repeating it over and over again. When we saturate our minds with God's word, we give the Holy Spirit a vocabulary to speak into our lives. I've also found that God gives me great insight into His word when I do not merely read it but instead take the time to dwell upon it. My favorite way to get close to God is to declare a silent retreat, taking a vow of silence for a day and going off to be on my own, typically surrounded by nature.

Many advisors are content to say "go pray" without giving further guidance, but after years of working with young people, I have found a little more direction on how to know your own heart and submit your relationship to God is often appreciated. When you pray, it is best to start by submitting the relationship to God's will by telling Him you want His will to be done despite what your heart wants. God wants His children to experience the joy of a good marriage, so ultimately His will for the relationship is also the best for you. Often we must first convince ourselves and decide that we indeed do want God's will more than our own. Honestly submitting to God's will is even harder to do after the relationship has already begun, so try to do it early (even before you go on a first date). You may also find that you have to return to this act, confessing your desire for His will to be done instead of your own.

As I mentioned earlier, my first serious dating experience was with a lady I courted for five years, and I had to go back to God after all that time and seriously declare that I wanted His will done instead of mine. It was because I honestly submitted to His will that I discovered I needed to stop courting her and move on, even though it was a very tough decision. My submission led to my finding Rebecca, and after just a few months of knowing Rebecca I was perfectly confident that she was someone God had intended for me.

After submitting to His will, you should ask God to enlighten you about your own heart. We often do not know what we really want, and it is important to ensure that we are not just seeking our own happiness but that we are really mature enough to give love and build a relationship. Men might find that they are really just desperate for physical touch, or women may discover that they love the idea of dating more than the actual person they are considering. In any case, ask God to reveal your real intentions and motivations, your heart's true desires, and ensure they are pure.

If the relationship has progressed, you may want to "fast, pray, and meditate for a day" asking God to reveal the character of the one you are courting. While He often doesn't speak as clearly to people as He did to me the first time I saw Rebecca, I have heard many stories of God revealing aspects of a person that indicated the relationship needed termination, or alternatively, that the other person was indeed in His will. You can also ask other people about the one you are considering to date/court/marry. Do not neglect seeking advice from your parents and siblings, who are often better judges of compatibility than are your friends.

While I have never tried it, I have often wondered about the wisdom of interviewing a potential courter's past girlfriend/boyfriend, and in one circumstance I advised it, and it turned out to be pivotal. The lady discovered the guy in question was less than virtuous, so she decided to refuse his advances. Of course, anything former girlfriends/boyfriends say must be taken with a grain of salt, and there is a chance that the person you are interested in may have learned from past mistakes. While I think there are times when this practice may make sense, you should realize that doing it will probably make your partner feel awkward or even feel a sense of betrayal. If you decide to interview a past girlfriend/boyfriend, I'd suggest you do not hide this fact but confess it to them since you do not want to breed mistrust.

If you drench the relationship in prayer but do not feel a tug for or against your pursuing it, what should you do? In my mind, if you are confident your own heart is in the right place, then you should be able to proceed with confidence. Submitting to God's will does not always result in His immediate confirmation to your heart that you should date someone, but it does seem that God's rejection of a relationship is quickly given when we submit to His will. This is because He wants to protect us from danger and allow us to make choices that help us mature. An example from my experience with my kids may be illustrative. If my son wants a book at a store that I do not like, I immediately and firmly reject it. However, I typically do not go out of my way to try to convince him which good book he should buy—I want that to be his own choice. Our heavenly Father likewise will keep you from danger if you submit to His will and ask for His leading in relationships.

How Do I know I'm in Love?

I knew I was in love when I realized I was ready to give completely to Rebecca, with no expectation of return, and despite all circumstances. This self-revelation was shocking and disquieting, and it even felt a little bit "out of control."

Simultaneously, it felt entirely natural—almost preordained and obvious. The feeling didn't arise all at once and it didn't strike me until we had been courting for a few months. Maybe it is because I am more of a cerebral person, but the realization that I loved Rebecca did not feel like an emotional compulsion so much as a self-illumination. I knew that I already was in love, and that this knowledge was just confirming to my mind what my heart had already decided.

Many people say they "just knew" when they met the right person. This certainly was my situation, only what I knew was that I would marry Rebecca—I did not feel I was in love with her at that time. I had the strange experience of figuring out how to court and fall in love with the one I knew I would marry. I remember returning home after first encountering her and praising God that He had selected such a beautiful person for me. I admit I was mostly thinking "Thank you for making her so beautiful on the outside." I didn't know her well enough to praise God for her wonderful personality, and I was glad God wanted me to marry someone I found extremely attractive rather than someone for whom I would have to look past her external appearance and see the beauty within. In my experience, God most often selects partners who are attracted to each other inside and out.

Can love happen in an instant? Studies show more men than women believe in love at first sight.[26] While I certainly think *some*thing can happen in an instant, I'm convinced many people who profess "just knowing" are actually guilty of selective memory modification. In retrospect, they "remember" just knowing, but had you asked them the day they met if they would marry each other, they would have been confused and befuddled. This is because love makes you feel the relationship is so natural that after a while you can't imagine yourself with anyone else, and it is easy to think that is how you always felt together.

You may or may not be someone who "just knows" instantly, so there are some things you can consider when attempting to understand your own heart. These points are not backed by scientific research (yet!) but simply constitute my own thoughts on the subject. I include them because they are common indicators of love, and I hope they will assist you to better interpret your own feelings. Keep in mind that no single point is conclusive in and of itself—just because you lack an area does not mean you are not in love.

First, you should have feelings. Love seldom occurs without them, though the presence of feelings alone is insufficient to diagnose love. Some people get goose bumps, or blush a lot, or get sticky palms. Heightened emotions in movies are often indicated by communication/brain glitches or awkward physical motions that look like the person forgot what they should do be doing with their arms or legs. While the emotions need not be so overwhelming as to reduce your mental abilities or impair your judgment, you should feel *something*. Furthermore, most people in love feel loss when saying goodbye, get butterflies in the stomach when looking forward to meeting, and often can't stop smiling in the other's presence.

Second, if you are in love you'll think about the other person when they are not around. You may just wonder if they made it to work okay or if they slept well. Sometimes almost everything you experience reminds you of your partner. When you love someone, you are truly concerned for their well-being, and you do not simply forget their existence when they are not in close proximity.

Third, a common trait for couples in love is that they feel compelled to tell the world about it. This ranges from crass graffiti on cement walls proclaiming "Mike Loves Sue" to a three-hour phone call telling your best friend all about how you met someone you like. People in love want to shout it from the mountaintops (or skyscrapers). Observers who are not romantically involved may interpret this as bragging or annoying, but real love simply wants to share its joy with all. This compulsion finds its greatest satisfaction in the wedding ceremony, where a couple gathers all their friends and family to witness their declaration of love and commitment.

Fourth, as discussed earlier, most often love starts by seeing the other person through rose-colored glasses. Everything they do or say is positive, and you strive to find connections and similarities. This may wear off with time, but the idea of giving the other the benefit of all doubt or wanting to trust them and exalt them should endure. If you find many things wrong with the other person, instead of rebuking yourself for being too judgmental, listen to that inner voice and acknowledge that you may not be compatible.

Fifth, love does not feel forced but in fact feels out of control. You should not feel like it is "hard work" to love— that leads to an almost unbearable load after marriage. Instead, you should be crazy for the other person, dedicated to them and feeling like you can't live without them. Most things in life must be mitigated, balanced, kept to appropriate levels—but not love. Just like we are to love the Lord our God with all our hearts all our minds and all our strength, I feel we should be exuberant in our love for our future spouse. Love is not of this world—it is not a quality of the finite but of the infinite, so it cannot be parceled out but must be given in full measure, pressed down and still overflowing. Ask yourself if yours is a generous love or if you are only giving it reluctantly or with great effort.

Finally, love often comes with great optimism. You may feel you are "on cloud nine" or that you can conquer the world. This is especially true when your love is reciprocated because you feel that if someone as special as they are likes you, you must indeed have great worth. I always wonder why we don't feel more of this in our relationship with God, for indeed it is true: if God loves me, I must have great worth.

While all these typical symptoms of love may be useful, in the end we chose to love or not to do so. Some people are easier than others to love, and some are probably easier than others to stop loving romantically. You need to ask yourself the question: am I willing to sacrifice myself to put his or her needs in front of mine, to put his or her welfare before mine, and to fulfill his or her wants instead of mine? If the answer is yes with reluctance, be careful. If the heart's answer is "of course," then you are probably on the right track.

How do you know they like you or are in love with you?

There may be many indicators, but I guarantee knowledge

of his (or her) love for you won't be found "in his kiss." Despite the popular song and cultural wisdom, lip collision offers little empirical data and no wisdom. In fact, you can't even trust how *you* feel about their physical touch or even romantic words. Our bodies may deceive us when it comes to evaluating how others feel. In the end love involves taking risk, and while you can never be certain the other person loves you, there are some intelligent things to consider.

For starters, you can look at the above criteria for discovering if you are in love and see if the other person demonstrates indicators of those factors. Do they appear to have feelings for you? Do they dread not being with you and think about you when you are apart? Do they go out of their way to see you? There are many nonverbal cues you can pick up on as well. Do they try to spend all available time with you? Do they look at you directly, face you straight on instead of looking at you sideways, look into your eyes more than they do with others, smile more, and laugh more when you're around? These all indicate attraction.

Perhaps the third indicator mentioned above is the most easy to test and may be the most useful in discovering if they love you or are just using you. What you must find out is if they tell others about their love for you, or do they just tell you all about it while keeping your relationship silent to others. Often their friends are full of clues as to whether or not they are really in love with you. If they keep the relationship private, it could be due to shyness or some other innocuous variable. However, there are many negative reasons why they might be trying to keep your relationship quiet. For example, maybe your partner is trying to get maximum self-gratification but is actually embarrassed about the relationship, thinking you are not worthy of them or that they are uncomfortable with you. A common male strategy is to just pull a lady along while still trying to "play the field," in effect looking for a "better option" to come along. These guys are hesitant to tell others about their current relationship, and will be especially careful to look "available" to other attractive women. The best situation is when you both love each other and want to tell the world about the gift of relationship.

Many people attempt to understand attraction by body language. In fact, some body language experts believe that while ladies have around 52 body language tells to show a man that they're interested, guys only have about 10 tells[27]. These include looking at you a lot, leaning your way, pointing hands/feet/toes toward you, and adjusting clothes to enhance his appearance such as smoothing a sweater or straightening a tie. Perhaps the clearest indicator here is excessive looking at you, as men are more visual and have a hard time prying their eyes away from a woman they are attracted to. You may also want to ask yourself the following questions that when answered positively may indicate that they like/love you:

1) Do they always give me the benefit of the doubt?

2) Would they let me win something—am I more important to them than a game?

3) Do they constantly look for ways we are a similar?

4) Do they have an almost idealized view of me (see me through rose-colored glasses)?

5) Will they defend me in front of others?

6) Do they tell their family and friends about me/us?

7) When we are together, do they give me their full attention (as opposed to acting easily distracted)?

8) Are they seeking a long-term relationship (or is there something else they want from me, as evidenced by their actions more than their words)?

9) Are they willing to sacrifice their wants/will for you? Is their love for you selfless or selfish?

10) Are they interested in things I am interested in simply because I am interested in them?

In the end there is no certain way to gauge if someone likes you. To love is to be willing to risk. You might have to resort to asking the person if they like you. This can be done by saying something like, "I feel attracted to you and have been impressed with what little I know about you. I'd like to get to know you better. I know you're busy, but would you be interested in exploring the possibility of a relationship?" This way you are flattering but not over the top, and you give the person the ability to say he or she is currently too busy as a nice way of letting you down. Note that if they say they are too busy, there is a 99% chance they are trying to decline and it has nothing to do with actually being busy. This wording also avoids the common problems of complementing only physical features or suggesting you are desperate.

Sometimes you just have to rely on your gut. I have found most couples who get married say they were mutually attracted to each other from the start, but there are also instances when one partner had to pursue the other for years before the attraction became mutual. If you feel the latter may be the case for you, be sure to read the chapter 6 on male-female communications differences, as men may need to learn how to take "the hint" and women may need to learn how to be more direct.

Avoiding the Path of Temptation

Assuming the attraction was mutual, and the courting has begun, one of the main areas of difficulty is always physical temptation. Before getting into the details of "how far is too far" it may be beneficial to lay some groundwork on sexual sin in general then look at a specific instance in the Bible when a godly man fell to temptation.

Let's be clear: God created sex, gave it to us in the context of marriage for our enjoyment and procreation, and best knows how sex should be used. Our society has taken this gift, perverted it, and in doing so truly opened Pandora's box and unleashed hideous consequences on our society. I'm convinced one reason so many people sleep around is that they find sex unfulfilling and think maybe if their partner were better looking, or maybe if they did a different technique, they would be satisfied. They are ridden by guilt and enslaved by their own lusts. They do not realize it is sex outside of marriage that is unfulfilling and laden with guilt and anxiety. In contrast, God intended sex to be a time of perfect freedom from guilt, of nakedness before a married partner without shame, and of love consummated rather than lustful taking.

It is the blessing of sexual enjoyment in marriage that

people desire, and they do not realize that having sex before marriage reduces its intended rapturous experience. This is because sin is never a productive or creative force; it doesn't make more pleasure, but it only twists a good thing and in the process destroys it. Sin involves taking something that is good and perverting it, typically for an immediate gain rather than allowing the good to bear full fruit. If there were no good in the world, and all we had was sin, we would not even want sin, because sin is only desirable because it steals the fruit of good. God's great gift to us of sex within marriage is destroyed when we take it out of the loving context of marriage and make it a thing of taking instead of giving, of selfishness instead of offering, of shame instead of transparency, and of lust rather than love. Sexual sin tears us apart, destroys us, and separates us from God.

Getting a bit more practical, sexual sin has its genesis in the body's natural desires. Our physical desire for sex and offspring and our psychological need to be loved and appreciated can provide fertile ground for sexual sin when we decide to meet our desires on our own terms instead of satisfying them appropriately.

While I admit sexual desire is a strong physical desire, it's real compulsion is created due to a sex-crazed culture that thrusts sex into the foreground and proclaims most forms of extra-marital sex as being acceptable and even expected behavior. It is astounding to think that as recently as the 1960s nearly every state had laws against sex outside marriage and that the military still has those laws though they are very selectively enforced. Our society has abandoned God's purpose for sex and even its own traditional wisdom on the subject, and as a society we are just beginning to reap the product of our disobedience and folly[28].

The path to sexual sin is fairly simple. Our bodies report a desire for sex, and our emotions act as gateways to convey the desire to our souls. The soul is the center of our personality, best conceptualized as an amalgamation of emotion, mind and will and not to be confused with our spirit, which can be thought of as conscience, intuition, and communion. In the soul our minds start playing with our desires and emotions, and that is where the battle rages between doing right and wrong. When we dwell on sin and do not take captive every thought, we start to strategize how we can sin and "get away" with it. While initial emotions and even temptation itself is not sin, I believe dwelling on sin and considering how it would feel or how we could "get away" with it is sin. Jesus exhorts us to not even lust in our hearts (Matthew 5), and we are joining forces with darkness when we do its job by tempting ourselves. The Bible and prayer assist us in this fight, informing us of God's desire for our purity and cleaning our hearts and minds. We sin when our mind ignores the Spirit and conceives of how to acquire the body's desire, then our will joins this rebellion and we decide to sin.

This path of sin is easy to observe in the first sin that happened in the Garden of Eden.

"Now the serpent was more crafty than any of the wild animals the LORD God had made. He said to the woman, "Did God really say, 'You must not eat from any tree in the garden?'" 2 The woman said to the serpent, "We may eat fruit from the trees in the garden, 3 but God did say, 'You must not eat fruit from the tree that is in the middle of the garden, and you must not touch it, or you will die.'" 4 "You will not surely die," the serpent said to the woman. 5 "For God knows that when you eat of it your eyes will be opened, and you will be like God, knowing good and evil." 6 When the woman saw that the fruit of the tree was good for food and pleasing to the eye, and also desirable for gaining wisdom, she took some and ate it. She also gave some to her husband, who was with her, and he ate it. 7 Then the eyes of both of them were opened, and they realized they were naked; so they sewed fig leaves together and made coverings for themselves." (Gen 3:1-7, NIV)

Here it is easy to see that the body desired food, the emotions found it pleasing to the eye, and the mind found it to be good for knowledge, so the will chose to sin then immediately decided to share the sin with another. Not every sin has its seed in a bodily need, but many of them do, and those are the sins that we must guard our minds against lest our minds team up with our emotions and convince our wills to sin.

Much like eating, the sexual drive is natural, so it can be difficult to harness when we are constantly tempted by it. Our society pushes sex on us at every turn, saturating the media and even becoming a real issue in daily public life due to ubiquitous advertising and immodest fashions. I'm convinced that the sexual drive is not as strong as most people think it is but that it has been reinforced to an almost compulsive level by its prevalence in our society. Just like a man surrounded by a cornucopia of deserts, snacks, and favorite foods would be tempted to eat even if he were not hungry, so we have flooded our culture with sex, making people constantly desire it. If we wish to tame this dragon we must cut it down to size by being very intentional about the movies and television we see, the books, magazines, and websites we view, and the music we listen to. By avoiding excessive sexual references we will reduce the temptation and give ourselves a fighting chance against sexual sin. We also must avoid being in the wrong places at the wrong times since that is exactly how King David, a man after God's own heart, fell into sin.

The Fall of the Godly

I did some things right and some things wrong in the area of sexuality before I was married. I recognize how hard it is to resist temptation, and I admire young people who are dedicated to purity. Being brutally honest I'd say I went too far physically, but to God's credit I never went "all the way" but instead was able to resist temptation and remained a virgin until I married (as was my bride). This confession is not meant to make people who have gone all the way feel bad but is made because I want to encourage young people that, in spite of what the voices of culture say, you, too, can succeed in staying pure sexually before marriage. Waiting until marriage to give yourself away sexually is by far the best plan, paying dividends in trust and healthy enjoyment.

For those who have failed to stay pure, I wish to stress that the issue is not virginity so much as purity. When we sin, we forever give up innocence, but thanks be to God He does not require us to become innocent (or a virgin) again but instead has provided a way for us to be granted His purity. "If we confess our sins, he is faithful and just and will forgive us our sins and purify us from all unrighteousness" (1 John 1:9). In fact, He loves us just as much after we confess as He loved us before we sinned. This does not mean there will be no lasting consequences (in damaged relationships and even potentially sexually transmitted diseases, which currently afflict one in two Americans by the age of 25[29]), but it does mean God ensures there are no eternal consequences and He repairs our most essential relationship with Him. When we sin then confess and repent, we do not become some kind of second class citizens in the Kingdom (sometimes people feel "just barely Christian"), but instead we are infused with a more powerful purity than we originally had, as it comes from God by faith and not from our own works. While sexual sin is more damaging than many other sins and is even against our own bodies (I Cor 6:18), it is miniscule compared to God's love and forgiveness.

In my own life I attribute much of my success in staying pure to having a sincere love for God, practicing a daily washing of myself in His word and His presence in prayer, and being dedicated to avoiding mass media that was sexually tempting. I went so far as to reject listening to songs I thought were too suggestive or spoke of a promiscuous lifestyle, and I avoided entirely (or, failing that, closed my eyes during) all visual content that was too sexual. I also set physical boundaries that were verbalized with my girlfriend and took responsibility as a man to ensure the relationship didn't go too far sexually rather than following the cultural norm and putting all the responsibility on the woman to slow down intimacy.

The need to establish boundaries is clearly illustrated by looking at the fall of King David, a man who was "after God's own Heart" but who gave it all up for a sexual encounter. Indeed, despite being elevated from shepherd to King and being granted more fame and riches than most of us can imagine, he succumbed to lust that resulted in adultery, murder, and eventually a rebellion that tore Israel apart. King David's path to perdition is instructive for us all, even as his forgiveness and re-elevation will stand for all time as a monument to God's unfailing love.

"Then it happened in the spring, at the time when kings go out *to battle*, that David sent Joab and his servants with him and all Israel, and they destroyed the sons of Ammon and besieged Rabbah. But David stayed at Jerusalem. Now when evening came, David arose from his bed and walked around on the roof of the king's house, and from the roof he saw a woman bathing; and the woman was very beautiful in appearance. So David sent and inquired about the woman. And one said, "Is this not Bathsheba, the daughter of Eliam, the wife of Uriah the Hittite?" And David sent messengers and took her, and when she came to him, he lay with her; and when she had purified herself from her uncleanness, she returned to her house. And the woman conceived; and she sent and told David, and said, "I am pregnant." (2 Samuel 11:1, NIV)

Notice that the time of year is given as "when kings go out to battle." David was a king—he should have been out leading his forces, but instead he stayed at home with little to occupy his time. There is a lot of wisdom in the old saying that "idle hands are the devil's." Probably one of the best ways to keep oneself pure is to be so busy doing good that you don't have time to sin.

Maybe even more applicable to our times is the fact that David was at the wrong place at the wrong time. He decided to stroll around his roof then spotted a woman bathing, probably because his roof was the highest around, so he could see where most others could not. Instead of recognizing the impropriety and looking away or leaving the roof entirely (in I Cor 6:18 we're told to actually flee sexual temptation), David stares, inquires about, and concocts a plan to sleep with her while her husband is off fighting David's war.

A big part of staying sexually pure is making wise decisions to avoid temptation in the first place. Like David, we too often are caught at the wrong place at the wrong time, and then we fail to flee the temptation. Many people I have counseled say that it was a "slippery slope" that they couldn't resist. They don't understand how they went too far. After all, they had only planned to go to a dance that involved a lot of slow contact then seclude themselves in a car in the dark to make out for awhile.

David's story has many other lessons for us, including the fact that sexual relations outside marriage often have dire consequences (ranging from pregnancy to STDs in our world). In our striving to hide our sin we often make things worse. David went so far as to have Bathsheba's husband murdered. Our sin can linger to affect those we love. Sin divided David's Kingdom and had many ramifications for his offspring.

While I did not find this principle in the Bible, I have learned a powerful way to resist sexual temptation. When tempted, I pray for the salvation of someone I know. This makes the temptation to sin remind me to pray, and when I pray, I find my priorities are set straight as I realize there are many more important things than gratification of sexual desires. From a spiritual warfare standpoint, I can see how this would frustrate the enemy. I imagine that he has a demon trying to keep someone from knowing God and a demon working on making me fall, but now the actions of the latter demon will lead to me praying, thus thwarting the actions of the former demon. While it may sound strange, I have found this a powerful way to resist temptation.

How far is going too far physically?

Nearly every time I speak on sexual topics I get this question, and the answer may surprise you. The Bible certainly condemns premarital sexual intercourse but avoids making a detailed list of taboo premarital sexual practices, other than the sexual practices that are always wrong such as bestiality (sex with animals), sodomy (anal intercourse), and incest (sex with close relatives). Instead, I feel it wisely speaks in generalities, admonishing us to remain pure, to flee sexual temptation, and to live holy lives. Most likely this is because the Holy Spirit can personalize boundaries for us, such that for some people avoiding nearly all contact is best, whereas for other couples a lot of physical interaction is possible. This is in no way saying God's word is relative or that a standard is not set, but is instead saying that while the Bible gives absolute moral law, the Holy Spirit often personalizes the law for us and makes it more stringent or clearer.

For example, the Bible clearly states that repeated drunkenness is wrong, but it does not suggest drinking any alcohol is wrong. Jesus' first miracle was turning water into wine, and Jesus was drinking wine[30] himself at the last supper. Still, some Christians feel God's will for them in our society is to abstain to be good examples to others (this is my practice). Others are recovering alcoholics and must never have another sip or else they could lose control, while still other Christians are comfortable drinking moderately and responsibly. All must follow the Bible's command to not drink to the point of being drunk, but beyond that all people should be convinced in their own minds and dedicated to obeying the law that the Holy Spirit has personalized for them. They also should be careful of judging others using their own standard—we only judge using the Bible's standard, allowing for differences that are created by the Holy Spirit for our own good.

In a way, the law of love frees us from the letter of the law but often simultaneously sets a higher (not a lower) standard.

To really love everyone would certainly mean following the law that is created to ensure we do not have disputes among ourselves, but it must also mean going a step further. If I love, I will not only avoid stealing but I will also give to the other person so they have no need to steal either. Love doesn't just follow the law; it perfects the law.

Similar to the alcohol example, some people can probably withstand higher levels of physical contact without sexual temptation than can others, but we are all clearly told to "flee from sexual immorality" (I Cor 6:18, NIV) rather than trying to endure it. Unlike every other sin that we are instructed to "stand" against, sexuality was created to naturally accelerate, so we are not supposed to flirt with it (yes, pun intended).

So what does it mean to "be holy" or "pure" or avoid "immorality?" The Hebrew society where these words were written was much more conservative than modern America. If we were to take the standards of those times as our own, we would probably have to avoid much of our daily culture to include watching commercials with scantily clad women or visiting beaches where often only a trivial amount of clothing hides the most private of parts.

I don't think we have to follow ancient sexual mores so much as our own. At the same time, we should acknowledge that our own standards of propriety have slid precariously in the last century. One hundred years ago preachers condemned the "new fangled" horseless carriages (cars) because they were difficult to climb in and out of without women being "indecent." By this they meant women exposed their ankles. In fact, boys used to hang around areas where women got out of cars just to catch a glimpse of their ankles, which was considered scandalous back then.

No one wants to go back to the ankle standard for long dresses or force women to wear full body suits to the beach, but we certainly need to be careful to "dress modestly" (I Tim 2:9) and should be aware that our sex-crazed culture is trying to pull us into sexual sin. Since our society is so sex-charged, it is wise to set very specific physical boundaries (such as "no touching above the knees") and to stick with them as your conscience directs. For the most part physical touch should be greatly limited while courting and may step forward some during an engagement period but even there must be kept in control so that it doesn't lead to intercourse or touching areas that are off-limits. Clearly any contact with genitals or breasts would be considered at least a "hint" of sexual immorality and thus should be avoided. Ephesians 5:3 sets the standard saying, "But among you there must not be even a hint of sexual immorality or of any kind of impurity or of greed, because these are improper for God's holy people." Please realize that these boundaries are for your own good. Indeed, progressing too far physically when dating can lead to tragedies like unintended pregnancy and Sexually Transmitted Diseases (STDs) and is guaranteed to lead to more difficult break-ups and emotional turmoil.

Probably the best way to know what is or is not acceptable is to realize you are dating the son or daughter of God and that our Father is watching you. You should never do anything physically that you do not wish Him to see because He does see it, and you have to deny His presence to do it. I remember making out with my girlfriend at a drive-in theater then seeing her parents were also on a date there. I decided to behave myself a bit more. Similarly, we all need to remind ourselves that God is always watching, and we should never do something to grieve the Holy Spirit.

Discussion of sexuality is never complete without saying a few words to those precious souls who have gone too far and live with that regret. I am saddened that the Church often speaks only of virginity and abstinence because I think it is often hurtful to people who are already beyond that ideal status. I realize that virginity and innocence are important, and abstinence is preached because it is the standard set by the Bible. I also strongly agree that by God's grace this standard is not too high (both my wife and I were virgins when we married), and I recognize that the consequences of premarital sin are so great that we must draw a line here and warn young people against sexual immorality.

However, the real issue is not innocence or virginity but purity. God doesn't reject people for the past they cannot change but offers everyone His forgiveness and purity by the power of His death and resurrection. In our society many young people have gone too far sexually and they feel condemned when we only preach of virginity and abstinence. Instead, let us also proclaim the truth of redemption. Our God's primary plan for humanity is redemption—He seeks and finds those who are lost and buys back those who are mortgaged to sin, He cleans, renews, and restores those who have fallen but seek forgiveness. Our God's love is so great that He accepts us with our dirt if we just come to Him, and thereafter He loves us by cleaning us off and making us His pure bride. If you have gone too far sexually already, realize that God is not done with you, has not written you off, and still has a plan to bless your life. Sexual sin doesn't stand a chance against the depth of God's love for you, and He already paid the price for your infidelity.

What we all must do is strive for sexual purity, whether it is initial purity by following abstinence or purity received by God's grace and forgiveness. Those who have fallen sexually should realize that like the recovering alcoholic they will have a much more difficult time remaining pure and should set more stringent standards for physical contact. It is worth the effort, as there are few things more powerful for a young marriage than being able to offer yourself in purity to the other.

Let me explain. One of the bulwarks of any marriage is trust. Without trust you end up second guessing each other, which feels like judgment and a lack of respect. If you both trust each other, it builds as you each feel it is important to live up to that trust. If you can deny a physical relationship outside of marriage with the person whom you eventually marry, it injects a powerful dose of trust into the relationship. After all, if you can resist sexual temptation with the person you loved so much that you married, you should be able to resist sexual temptation with anyone else. We therefore must strive to live lives of purity, and while abstinence and innocence are by far the best plan, sexual purity (both virginity and through forgiveness and subsequent abstinence) is the real issue and one of the most precious gifts you give your spouse and future relationship.

In conclusion, we have seen some things that will help us know our own hearts and evaluate the hearts of others. We also understand that we need to hear from God to know our own hearts. While love is a decision, and we can decide to love anyone, there are many things suggested here to assist us in knowing if we are ready to make a real decision to love. Furthermore, we have looked at sexual temptation and learned to set boundaries to prevent the physical relationship from robbing us of some of the joy that comes from courting. We have also stressed the importance of purity, which leads to trust. In the next chapter we'll look at how men and women are equal but very different and how leadership works in relationships.

CHAPTER FIVE FURTHER LEARNING

1) Have you ever been in love? How did you know?

2) How will YOU know when you are in love?

3) What physical boundaries will you set in romantic relationships?

4) What was the lesson you most appreciated from the story of David's temptation?

CHAPTER 6

Male and Female He Created Them:
Gender Equality and Leadership

"There are two theories to arguing with a woman. Neither works."
— *Will Rogers*

We do not know how long Adam was alone in the garden simply enjoying creation and the presence of God. There is a good chance that it was a long time. Contrary to many overzealous renaissance painters' illustrations, the Genesis narrative suggests Adam was alone when God gave the instruction to abstain from eating fruit from the "tree of the knowledge of good and evil," and much more time could have gone by naming all the animals before he started feeling alone. Eventually, even surrounded by such glorious nature and with the company of God, Adam felt incomplete. I think he was made in God's image to such an extent that he had too much love and needed an object of his love who was not able to be controlled but could freely decide to return that love. In any case, just like many young men today feel incomplete without a girlfriend, Adam seems to have felt something was lacking. That loneliness led God to give Adam the task of naming all of the animals. I imagine that task took a considerable amount of time since Adam didn't just spout syllables but probably took the time to really observe each animal in order to give it an appropriate name. Indeed, Adam was not just trying to get through a labeling exercise but was, in fact, also trying to find a compatible companion. In the end, however, no suitable helper was found. In Genesis 2:18-3:1 the Bible explains the solution to this conundrum:

> "The LORD God said, "It is not good for the man to be alone. I will make a helper suitable for him." Now the LORD God had formed out of the ground all the beasts of the field and all the birds of the air. He brought them to the man to see what he would name them; and whatever the man called each living creature, that was its name. So the man gave names to all the livestock, the birds of the air and all the beasts of the field. But for Adam no suitable helper was found. So the LORD God caused the man to fall into a deep sleep; and while he was sleeping, he took one of the man's ribs and closed up the place with flesh. Then the LORD God made a woman from the

rib he had taken out of the man, and he brought her to the man. The man said, "This is now bone of my bones and flesh of my flesh; she shall be called 'woman, 'for she was taken out of man." For this reason a man will leave his father and mother and be united to his wife, and they will become one flesh. The man and his wife were both naked, and they felt no shame." (NIV)

As was mentioned in Chapter 3, it is important to note that Eve was made from a rib taken from Adam's side. Eve was not made from Adam's head to rule over him, nor from his feet to be trodden over by him, but from his rib to be a companion and equal with him. But this begs the question: why did God make an Eve instead of a Steve? That is, why did God decide that Adam should share his love with an entirely new creation (the female), instead of simply putting another male in the Garden to be Adam's buddy? Since most likely the reader is between 15 and 30, your immediate answer may be sexually driven, but that is not it at all—okay, maybe it is part of the equation, but it is not the most important part. The important part is that Adam needed a creature different from himself in order to be complete. While men and women are equals, they are also different and complementary and certainly were never created to be the same.

Different but Equal

The concept of different but equal is hard to grasp. If you are familiar with history, this concept may remind you of how after the Civil War many southern states passed laws that said blacks and whites were "separate but equal." In reality the laws granted whites privileges and kept blacks oppressed—there was no real equality at all. It is a sad testament to human frailty that it took the Civil Rights Movement of the 1960s, a full seven decades after slaves in the United States had been freed, to amend this intolerable situation.

We have a hard time understanding separate but equal or different but equal, so our society often over-emphasizes male and female similarity in order to better promote equality. Though the goal is noble, the act is pure folly. Not only are the two genders very different biologically, hormonally, and behaviorally, but also men do not want women to act like men just as women do not want men to act like women.

Most of the confusion comes from a lack of understanding how value is derived. We do not have value because we are tall, strong, pretty, smart, or smell nice. Indeed, there is no quality we possess nor action we can accomplish that changes our value. That is because a thing's value is not an intrinsic quality but something granted to it by its creator or owner.

Think about it. You can decide to prize or despise the things you own or create. If you create works of art, you can like one more than the other or destroy one and display the other. The creator decides the value of his or her creation. Similarly, even as the U.S. Constitution attests, we are endowed by our Creator with inalienable rights. The reason we are equal is not because it is written in the Constitution, but because the Creator loves us equally, so the Constitution simply testifies to that fact.

If you erase the creator, you also erase value. People who do not believe in God cannot grasp two things being of equal value while being different, so they insist the two things are the same so that they can have equal value. However, in God's economy there is great diversity and yet equality. In truth, no two individuals are really "equal" in any dimension if we just have an accurate enough instrument to measure it. We are all different heights, different levels of intelligence, different levels of strength, smell different, etc. If our attributes had to be the same to be equal, we could never be equal. However, we can have equality because our Creator has decided to love us all equally. Perhaps the only way we are truly *absolutely* equal is that we are all equally loved by our Creator. God so loved the world that He gave His only Son for its redemption—He loves us all completely (and unlike some of us He doesn't have to run through mental exercises and check lists considering if He really loves us or not!).

This is quite freeing. It means men and women can have great differences and can have space to be themselves; in no way does that mean we are unequal. It means we can play different roles and still retain equality. A great exemplar of this ideal was Jesus Himself. On earth Jesus submitted to the Father completely, even saying that He only did what the Father in Heaven told Him to do. "Jesus gave them this answer: 'I tell you the truth, the Son can do nothing by himself; he can do only what he sees his Father doing, because whatever the Father does the Son also does.'" (John 5:19, NIV). Furthermore, Jesus limited His omniscience while on earth, meaning He didn't know everything like God does. Jesus said, "'Heaven and earth will pass away, but my words will never pass away. No one knows about that day or hour, not even the angels in heaven, nor the Son, but only the Father.'" (Mark 13:31-32, NIV). Despite these clear differences that arose from Jesus' having in humility emptied Himself of His divine powers (Phil 2:6), Jesus and God were of course equal. The persons of the trinity may take on different roles, but for all that they remain equal in value.

Similarly, men and women have different characteristics and roles but remain of equal value. The Bible clearly intends for men to be the spiritual leaders in the home and church. By "leader" I mean servant-leader, the ones who out-serve and assist others (see Eph 5: 23)[31]. Men are not supposed to lead the family by coming home in 1950s fashion, kicking up their feet and being served by their wives. To the contrary, the Bible instructs us that to lead is to serve, and that to be strong means to help the weak and not lord it over them. The best leaders out-serve their followers.

If I am the leader in the home, then my job is to out-serve my wife, to lead by example, to have vision for my family, and to provide for its future. While every major decision is made by both Rebecca (my wife) and me, in the end the responsibility for the outcomes falls squarely on my shoulders. My job is to discover what my wife and family want (or need) then make self-sacrificial decisions to lead them where they want to go or in a very few circumstances, lead them where it is best for them to go despite what they want. While the husband may be the leader, his job is to lead where the wife wants to go. In this manner the husband brings glory to God by leading in a selfless manner, and the wife brings glory to God by submitting to her husband's leadership, and both are blessed by each other. In this relationship there is no fight for power and no role confusion—only harmony and glory.

One characteristic that greatly assists men in their leadership role is that they often have fewer preferences than women. Whether it is because they simply have no strong preferences or they just don't know what they prefer, most men are willing to do what women want simply because there is no competing alternative. While women may have opinions about a myriad of day-to-day topics and often know where they want to go or what they want to do, men often don't care what is going on and only hold strong convictions about less mundane issues (ranging from politics and religion to sports, which they often consider important and not mundane). Men can thus concentrate on discovering what the woman wants to do and agree to do it without being overly tempted to lead selfishly and only do what they want to do. Leaders with fewer preferences have an easier time listening to followers and satisfying the followers' desires first.

I will resist digressing here into marriage roles and the beauty of service and instead stay discussing the pre-marriage situation, but I hope to return to the topic of the marriage relationship in much more depth in a subsequent book entitled *Adam and Eve Meet Marriage.* For now, let me conclude this topic with a simple short story to drive home the point that Christian role division and specialization in no way demeans either gender and that Christianity certainly doesn't devalue women.

I often take plane rides around the country to speak at various seminars and conferences, and on one trip I sat beside a very modern-looking young lady who had quite fashionable clothing and shortly-bobbed blonde hair. We engaged in pleasant conversation that eventually revealed she was very opposed to Christianity because she thought it was patriarchal and oppressive to women. I told her that simply isn't true and that her statement could easily be falsified simply by looking around the world to discover the true plight of women. I've traveled to about 50 countries on six continents, and I can say with some certainty that when you compare the value recognized and freedoms granted women in countries with Christian cultural heritages with countries where no Christian heritage exists it quickly becomes evident that Christianity has liberated women. Christianity may not have always acted toward women as it should, but it assuredly has treated women better than any other religious system. In fact, Jesus and the Apostle Paul elevated women to extraordinary counter-cultural roles in the early church, and the Bible's instructions about roles in no way oppresses women but, in fact, frees them to be themselves.

The young lady was shocked and admitted that she had never heard the other side of the argument. Having overcome that initial prejudice against Christianity, we then engaged in an outstanding conversation about God that resulted in her praying and confessing Jesus as her Savior.

Male Leadership in Dating Relationships?

As mentioned in chapter 2, the sinister aspects of our

culture have been waging a war on masculinity for half a century, and unfortunately today it is difficult to find healthy, mature men who can lead a family or even a date. Men are told to be more nurturing and "like women" from the feminist movement while Hollywood shows the wolfish lone-killer macho man as the paragon to emulate. Men are told on one hand to be gentlemen and practice chivalry then on the other hand get reprimanded by hyper-feminists for small things like holding doors open. I will never forget holding the door open for a female cadet at the Air Force Academy on a cold blustery day only to be accosted for chauvinism once we got inside. These days men are told so many conflicting messages that they often capitulate to lethargy and self-centric tendencies, behaving like the masculine buffoons portrayed on most sitcoms.

While there is no doubt that women like different things in a man, I am convinced the vast majority of women (and nearly all mature Christian women) prefer men who are strong, selfless, and have the ability to lead. But what does leadership look like in a dating relationship?

As mentioned earlier, I think men are the most natural initiators in relationships, though women should not feel bad about initiating if the guy is not taking hints. In general, it is the man's job to "break the ice" since that job is undesirable and takes some courage. A real man can risk rejection and can "put himself out there" to lead a conversation to the deeper levels as discussed in earlier chapters. A real man can also read the nonverbal hints a disinterested woman exudes and has the self-confidence to back off rather than plunging forward and making a fool of himself. But leadership in dating goes far beyond just navigating the initial stages.

Even if it is unconscious, eligible ladies are looking for a man they can respect, who will raise their children well, and who will be devoted to her. They want a man who is a hard worker so he can provide for the family, who is concerned for her welfare before his own (which is the core of chivalry— putting others above self), and essentially who can lead in the relationship.

Leadership in a dating relationship involves setting priorities as a spiritual leader, establishing physical boundaries, and even planning most of the dates. Men should take the lead by not giving in to frivolous impulses but instead stressing the importance of long-term duties such as finishing homework before dating or not skipping out on work. The man should show mature judgment rather than being swayed by emotions of the moment—while the woman may whine about the decision, in the end she will be more impressed by his discipline and wisdom. While an occasional romantic streak of spontaneity and shirking of duties may be allowed, a good relationship leader tries to look at the larger picture and act for the long-term good of both people rather than making a fleeting short-term decision that may result in dire consequences later.

Much has been written about spiritual leadership in dating, but I think the concept is more for marriage. Until marriage or moving out of the home, parents retain spiritual leadership roles. In my experience dating spirituality can be too intimate and is largely out of place between a man and woman until marriage or at least engagement. The man's role as spiritual leader is therefore reduced to respecting the father's role as spiritual head over his date, to establishing the beginnings of a spiritual relationship, and to encouraging church attendance rather than trying to work on his date's spiritual maturity by himself.

I would even go so far as to say a couple would be wise not to do Bible studies together or pray a lot alone together while just dating, but they can and should experience spiritual situations with each other while participating in church functions. The man should lead here by insisting on regular church attendance and being dedicated to participation in church activities, rather than attempting to lure his lady out of Christian fellowship. The woman should, of course, evaluate her man's spiritual maturity and take that into account, but she should be more impressed by his willingness to submit to other godly authorities than by any quasi-rebellious tendencies to pull her away from Church fellowship (even for the ostensibly righteous purpose of doing Bible studies alone as a couple).

Counter to most cultural messages, I also feel the man should lead when it comes to restricting physical intimacy. It is not the lady's responsibility alone to protect her virtue, but instead the man should be adamant about ensuring the relationship doesn't progress too far physically. He can do this by initiating discussions on how far is too far and by ensuring he does not try to seduce his lady or put them both in compromising situations. If the man really loves, he should recognize saving physical intimacy for marriage is the best route for both partners. In the end, these decisions will impress the lady more than any sloppy romantic encounter that often engenders feelings of guilt and remorse. In fact, staying pure, upright and blameless will lead to many more rewards after marriage as there will be increased desire and satisfaction in sexual activity.

Clearly the leadership role of planning dates is also important, and wisdom must be used to not place yourself in compromising situations. While there is nothing wrong with women planning dates, and in fact that should be encouraged, too, men would do well to realize planning dates is a powerful way to demonstrate creativity and express romantic love. Planning dates should not be a burden but should be an exciting experience—a kind of "event-gift" you get to give your paramour. It is important to not only plan where to go but also give some thought as to what conversation topics may be entertained, and we will discuss both these issues more in-depth in chapters 7 and 8.

Leading All the Way to Lunch

Perhaps the best way to demonstrate the kind of leadership men should take in a dating relationship, and the distinct differences between the way genders communicate is to describe a typical situation in which a couple wants to go out to eat but can't decide where to go. Jack wants to be with Jill and knows that sharing a meal is the culturally appropriate thing to do, so he asks her if she wants to go out to eat. Jill replies with a neutral-sounding "sure" even though her heart is leaping at the thought of a date with Jack. Jack then asks, "Where do you want to go?" Jill responds with: "I don't care;

where do you want to go?" Jill wants to respect Jack's intent and doesn't know what kind of date he wants—is it romantic or just as friends? Does he want fine dining or fast food? Is there a price range she should be careful about?

Jill's response was not at all what Jack was hoping to encounter. He is more interested in Jill than the food—he'd eat just about anywhere if it involved being in her company. He wants her to know this fact, and he wants her to be pleased with where they go, so he replies, "I don't care; where do you want to go?"

Now it's Jill's turn for consternation—Jack hasn't given her anything to work with. She decides to stay consistent with her first response and says again, "I don't care; where do you want to go?"

Having heard "I don't care" twice from Jill, Jack decides maybe she feels just as he does—it doesn't matter where they go as long as they are together. Well, we might as well go somewhere close and inexpensive then, he decides. That way we can do more dates in the future. "How about Subway?" he asks with the beginning of a smile.

Jill feels let down. Subway! Really? How is that romantic? It is right near campus and wouldn't really be getting away together. "I'd rather not go there," she says a bit timidly.

Jack is taken aback and his smile vanishes. She obviously doesn't feel as he does that just the company alone is good enough. He is also confused—isn't she contradicting herself? "But you said you don't care," he states more as a question than a declaration. Jill realizes the words she said certainly meant that, but doesn't see why Jack can't understand what she meant—what she really was saying is: "Pick a nice place that I like" and not really "Anything will do."

This scenario plays out countless times across the globe because men and women do not understand each other well enough. The problem involves communication (women hint at things whereas guys are more explicit), food desires (guys sometimes really don't care what they eat whereas while women may not know where they want to go, they almost always have some places in mind they do not wish to go), opinions (women almost always have one whereas men sometimes don't even know what their opinion is at any given time). At its root is the proper role of male leadership in a relationship. ***It is the man's job to lead the woman where she wants to go and to know and love her enough to understand her desires.*** Women tend to have more opinions/desires than men, but they want the man to lead them and make decisions. Studies have repeatedly shown that making decisions takes energy[32], and women would prefer that men make the decision and accept any unforeseen consequences. However, the man realizes he has fewer opinions/desires and therefore thinks the woman (who actually has an opinion) should lead them to what she wants, or at least tell him explicitly where he should take her.

Instead of getting caught in the infinite loop of "I don't care; where do you want to go?" there is a great solution that takes into account the differences between genders. Instead of leaving the location open-ended, what if Jack decides to make some suggestions. He begins with, "Well, we can go to Subway or Panera Bread, or there is an Olive Garden not too far away." Now Jill knows the parameters of the date, and having limited options helps her make her choice. However, being a woman, Jill still avoids an explicit decision. Instead, she responds with a description of her feelings. "They have great salads at Olive Garden," she says.

Here is where many man fail to lead and put the discussion right back into the same downward spiral. Most uninformed men would take the statement at face value rather than perceiving it as a hint upon which to act. These men would fall into the trap of putting the onus back on the woman by saying, "Oh, so you want to go to Olive Garden?" That makes the woman have to lead, have to decide, and have to check her taste buds again to see if the statement is accurate.

But our newly informed Jack reads into Jill's hint and makes a wiser decision. "Great—I like Olive Garden. Let's go there," he responds with resolve. Jill happily agrees, glad to be free from the responsibility, and knows that if for some reason the salad isn't good at Olive Garden, it isn't her fault—Jack made the decision to go there.

The quintessential thing to remember about this dialogue isn't just how to settle lunch plans (though being a man I agree that is important!) but instead note how each partner approached the situation. Men often give up talking to women because they feel they are being toyed with or not taken seriously. They wonder why the woman can't just come out and say what she wants rather than talking in circles. Some men go so far as committing the cardinal sin in relationships with women: they give up trying to understand them.

Men, every time a lady seems confusing because she is only

giving hints instead of being more blatant, think of it as a puzzle that you need to figure out. She is not intentionally trying to confound you, but instead she is giving you an opportunity to show her how much you care for her. If you are willing to learn what she wants, to understand how she thinks, to know her well enough that you take the time to discover what her hints mean, it is a powerful statement about how interested you are in her. If you care for her, you will enjoy puzzling out her meaning, and exploring her mystique. If you give up quickly, you are basically telling her she is not important enough to know—that you were after her for your own purposes rather than being truly interested in her for her own good. In many ways a better test cannot be devised to ensure selfish men have a hard time getting dates.

This principle, of course, applies to many more situations than just trying to find a place to eat. In general, women are used to communicating with other women, and among them being blunt is almost rude or crude. A woman being blunt with another woman can even be taken as an insult because it is like saying the receiver is too dumb to figure out the obvious. Women are used to reading into each other's behavior and fluently interpreting nonverbal communication. They are therefore often baffled at how intelligent guys can't get simple messages, and they don't want to insult a potential paramour by being too obvious. They are also worried about seeming to be too forward, so they think hints are the best way to initialize relationships. Many times I have heard college ladies in my office complain about how they can't understand why the guy they are chasing won't take a hint or doesn't even know they exist. What makes the situation comical is that many of the guys would love to be courting the lady if they just thought they had a chance to do so, but they truly never interpreted the lady's hints as being romantic interest.

One of the more common ways this confusion is circumvented is through friends. Especially in high school it seems common for a lady to tell a guy that her friend likes him, instilling in him the courage and confidence he needs to initiate a conversation with the friend and potentially start a relationship. Another way for things to work is that the woman simply becomes increasingly obvious until the guy understands her meaning and sends off signals of his own indicating that he is or is not interested. If we were all fluent in the language of hints, it might make the world a more pleasant place as we could avoid blatant rejection. However, since we live in the real world, being increasingly obvious or relying on friends may be the only paths forward.

Multiple studies have confirmed that men are not as good as women at both encoding and decoding nonverbal cues[33]. Men don't catch hints very well and are harder to read since their own thoughts and emotions are less telegraphed in their faces and body positions. Women are socialized from a young age to play games like patty cake, hand-clapping games and looking deeply into each others' faces. Their games and intense interest areas tend to be about family and relationships, whereas the boys are outside chasing each other with sticks or inside playing the latest video game that typically portrays anything but social behavior.

The one curious exception to this rule is that women have

been found to be less accurate at detecting deception[34]. One hypothesis is that women overlook deception in order to be more polite. While women of course have the ability to decode nonverbal cues of lying, they tend to turn off this skill in polite deference to the speaker[35]. Another possibility is that women expect more embellishment than men and confuse outright deception cues, or that men are simply more suspicious of deception and are more aware when it is present. Then again, maybe the research is flawed and the folk wisdom of Oscar Wilde is more accurate, as he once wrote, "A man's face is his autobiography. A woman's face is her work of fiction."

In this chapter we looked at gender equality and the leadership role in dating relationships. Real value is based on the creator's assessment, and men and women can be content that they are both loved equally because they are both loved absolutely by a God who would rather die than live without them. Since equality does not necessarily imply similarity, men and women can serve in different roles and still be equal. In general, it is the man's role to lead where the woman wants to go. Leadership in relationships means out-serving the other person.

It turns out that there are many more differences between men and women that need to be understood if we are to have a modicum of harmony in our relationships, and while some of our differences are learned, many of them have their genesis in biology. In the next chapter we'll look more in-depth at the differences in communication patterns between men and women, and we'll exam some of the biological roots to our behaviors that have a tremendous impact on all our inter-gender relationships.

CHAPTER SIX FURTHER LEARNING

1) What is your favorite thing, and why is it valuable to you?

2) Male leadership in relationships is a Biblical concept, but sometimes it clashes with our society. Why is male leadership under assault in our culture?

3) One characteristic of men that helps make their leadership role easier is that they typically have fewer preferences than women. What are some other characteristics of men that might assist them in being good leaders?

4) If men are to be leaders in the family, what about in the church? What does the Bible say about this topic?

5) Do you believe it is possible to be different but equal? Why is this such a difficult concept?

CHAPTER 7

Adam Isn't Eve: Communication and Biological Differences

"Women like silent men. They think they're listening."
— *Marcel Achard*

God clearly never intended Adam and Eve to be the same. Instead, He wanted Adam and Eve to complement each other, being different yet still in love. God designed marriage to be one man and one woman, and even though later in the Old Testament polygamy was allowed, it is interesting to note that nearly all of the men actually were in love with one wife in a special way (for example Abraham had Sarah, Jacob had Rachel, and David had Bathsheba). Choosing the right mate is not about picking someone who is exactly like you, but is instead about having someone to complete you, who balances you out and who can round your rough edges. No matter who you date or marry, you will find there are plenty of differences simply because men and women are not the same. This chapter focuses on those differences with the hope that understanding each other better will lead to an appreciation of our differences and enhanced interactivity.

Communication Differences

Communication researcher Dr. Deborah Tannen has studied inter-gender communications for decades, and in her book *You Just Don't Understand*[36] she concludes that one of the best ways to understand the differences between male and female communication is to see that men use "report talk" whereas women use "rapport talk." Men prefer to communicate in a succinct manner, getting to the point in the first sentence or two and linearly building their points. Their main purpose in communicating is to gain power, so they will switch the subject when it is an area that is unfamiliar to them and they have no problems interrupting in order to display their knowledge or expertise. In fact, men frequently interrupt and compete for airtime, so they are less bothered by others interrupting them. Furthermore, men will seldom confess ignorance or ask advice for a problem (especially from a woman) because that may show weakness.

On the other hand, women use "rapport talk" and focus on building relationships. They freely demonstrate their ignorance or weaknesses as they realize that through vulnerability they can build common ground and understanding. Rather than trying to quickly get to a point, female communication is characterized by sharing information to help others gain the same level of knowledge and/or feelings as the speaker has. Women may thus talk in circles or even have no real "point" to the communication. One major difference and point of contention is that women typically wait to speak until others are fully heard, and they expect to be able to finish their sentences uninterrupted. Interrupting a woman is like stating that she is not important enough to be understood—a message no man should dare to send.

The two sexes even differ in their motivation to listen, as women listen in order to empathize and think or feel as the speaker does, whereas men listen in order to act. This listening difference shows itself in many situations. Men will often go with a trial-and-error problem solving pattern whereas women will often opt for a discussion of all possibilities before acting.

I often take communications field trips to New York with students in the summer, and comparing two situations in New York may best illustrate some of these communication differences. One year I had 12 ladies and 4 guys, and we were trying to decide what Broadway show to see on a Thursday night (when tickets are available to most shows). Everyone wanted to make the decision quickly, buy the tickets, and go shopping until the show. After a half hour of the ladies discussing the situation and trying to ensure no one would be left out or upset by the group's decision, the guys interjected that they were tired of waiting and that they would start walking toward one of the theaters. The ladies were a bit upset since they had not yet come to emotional consensus on where they should go, but once the guys started walking, they hurried on behind them and redoubled their efforts to figure out where they all should go. Since they were forced into action, they arrived at a decision before the guys arrived at a destination, and then they directed the guys to their desired theater. In truth, the guys had no clue where they were going, and they even passed the theater that would eventually be their final destination. To them, various shows were equally desirable, and they just wanted to act to get the decision made so they could get on with the rest of the evening.

While I thought that event was a bit amusing, it didn't really hit me as a great example of inter-gender relations until the following year when I had 8 ladies and no men in the group. Some students including all the guys had to bail out of the trip at the last moment due to understandable financial issues. This time the scenario repeated itself, except that there were no males to start walking. The group thus debated for *two and a half hours* until even my academic interest was lost, and I just said, "We'll figure it out on the way" and started walking. While I fully understood what was happening, in the end I was just too male to let the debate continue without action. I also like to think I was showing them mercy by forcing activity. Sure enough, on the road the ladies came up with a plan that made everyone happy then took over directing me to the desired theaters.

Every semester I teach two classes on inter-gender communication and I always split the class into gals and guys and ask them to discuss questions about communication. The first question is "What do you least like about the other gender's communication?" Almost every year both men and women respond with "They can't communicate!" What is truly hilarious is that both groups mean something completely different even when they are saying the exact same words.

The ladies typically mean that men cannot express themselves. When they probe a guy for conversation, they discover guys can't say what they feel about things and that men often evade conversation and use single syllable answers or even just grunts. Since women nearly always know what they feel about just about everything (they have a much stronger internal awareness due to brain differences that we will discuss later in this chapter), they feel guys are refusing to communicate when they give answers like "I don't know," "I don't care," and "so what?" I think most men simply have fewer preferences than women, and even how they have a preference they often need time to discover exactly what they feel about something.

I have repeatedly observed how this leads to trouble. The woman asks what a guy thinks about a certain subject and is dissatisfied with his non-answer, so she pushes further. The guy responds by wondering what it is she wants him to say, so he invents a position and gives that to her hoping it will make her happy. The lady then reads the guy's nonverbal cues and suspects the guy is lying, so she gets even more upset at his lack of sincerity and suspects the worst from his real opinion of the subject. This in turn makes the guy upset since he was simply trying to accommodate her and really has no opinion on the matter whatsoever.

When the guys in class say women can't communicate, they mean that women talk in circles too often, hint at things too much, and refuse to get to the point. They feel women make communication harder than it needs to be and wish for women to simply say what they want and be more blatant. To them, women are coy and even dishonest, and they see too many words as confusing. In fact, one of the best ways to frustrate a man is to make a short story long or to speak for 3 minutes or more without getting to a discernible point.

When I was young, naïve, and newly married, I remember a time where I was in a hurry, and my wife started one of these kinds of stories. Since I knew it would not end anywhere important and I didn't want to let down the college/career group I was leading that night, I interrupted her and asked if I could get "the Cliffs Notes version." Rebecca looked at me in astonishment then burst into tears, and I had to spend two hours telling her I meant no disrespect and that I valued her and her stories and that I'd do a better job of listening in the future. I should have saved her emotions and my time by simply listening and thinking to myself, "This is just another way I can say 'I love you' to my wife."

There are, of course, many more differences between men and women that I can't cover in their entirety here. For instance, men consistently express that they "like" conversation, whereas women report that they "need" it. Women ask three times more questions in mixed company, and when in segregated groups women use more words per minute than groups of men, but in mixed groups men actually dominate the speaking time, mostly because they are willing to interrupt. Women are culturally programmed to smile more, but they also are prone to take negative comments much more seriously and will search for some nugget of truth even in the most obvious and insincere teasing joke.

Some experts have even proposed that women must use thousands of words more per day, and this causes problems in traditional one income homes (a dying phenomena in our culture) because after work the husband has spent all of his words, and the wife is just warming up to adult conversation. Though the data to support this contention seems scant (solid communications studies have not found a real difference in the number of words used per day), it has led to some interesting debates and stories[37].

For instance, there is the husband who looked through a newspaper and came upon a study that said women use more words than men. Excited to prove to his wife that he had been right all along when he accused her of talking too much, he showed her the study. "Men use about 15,000 words per day, whereas women use 30,000 a day," it said. The wife thought for an instant, then told her husband "That's because we have to repeat everything we say." The husband replied, "What?"

While the differences between men and women are legion, we somehow have been getting along well for thousands of years, so there must also be many similarities. Furthermore, the wisdom of the ages suggests that groups are optimized when they include both men and women, so somehow their differences enhance groups rather than detracting from them. I strongly feel that the differences between the sexes are created so that we perfectly balance each other: We not only like each other, but in many ways we need each other to function optimally.

Biological Differences

Where do all these differences originate? Are they culturally-conditioned, or is there a deeper reason that men and women do not communicate the same way? Some cultural variability is clear as many of the accepted ways to behave are actually modeled by our society or inculcated through the socialization process. However, most of our differences can now be traced to our biology, as men and women experience the effects of genes, biochemical processes, hormones, etc.

Other than physical brain differences, the main culprits for our differences are dopamine, serotonin, estrogen, and testosterone. It is important to realize that hormones, especially testosterone, differentiate the sexes early on because they powerfully affect the early development and organization of the brain. This means nature trumps nurture because all future interactions will be processed on differently "wired" brains.

Perhaps the biggest reason males and females behave and communicate differently is the amount of testosterone flowing through their systems. Studies suggest men have between 10 and 100 times more testosterone than women at any given time, making them significantly more aggressive, willing to take risks, and prone to violence. In his article *Why Do Men Act The Way They Do?*[38], Andrew Sullivan explains men are flooded with the testosterone hormone in the uterus a few weeks after conception, during the first few months after birth, and again during puberty. Throughout life men consistently have about ten times more testosterone in their systems than women, which " … profoundly affects physique, behavior, and mood."

As mentioned in Chapter 2, this may be why men are more willing to initiate relationships and risk rejection.

Testosterone is also a key player in the finding that males are generally more violent and aggressive than females, comprising 86% of U.S. incarcerations for violent crimes[39]. There is even evidence that men with higher levels of testosterone have a higher chance of criminal behavior and that a large percentage of women in prison for violent crimes actually committed their crimes during their premenstrual cycle when lower levels of estrogen made them more male-like hormonally[40].

Multifarious brain differences provide insight into gender differences, even after taking into account the fact that the average male brain is 10% larger than the average female brain. It should be noted here that the brain size difference does not correlate to intelligence differences because males also have a larger average body mass that takes more brain space to control. Men have proportionately larger brain centers for action and aggression, whereas the female brain actually has a larger center that regulates aggression and anger (including a larger cingulate gyrus). This means that it is generally easier to anger a man than a woman and that men can lose control easier[41].

This may also account for differences in listening patterns because men typically listen in order to act whereas women listen in order to empathize (feel the speakers' feelings). Typically men want every communication to have a point, and they are frustrated when they cannot easily derive a point and thereby get a clue about what they should do or say next.

Women are often content to "just chat" and attempt to better understand each other. Men also are driven to act in leadership situations and are much more likely to adopt a "trial and error" process than women who prefer a fully developed plan (having considered all alternatives and developed contingency plans) before proceeding.

Maybe a quick anecdote will help illustrate this difference. When we buy new technology for our home, such as a computer or flat screen TV, I immediately go about setting it up without any thought for the instruction manual. Typically about half way through the process my wife meanders over and decide to rip the manual out of its plastic cover and start browsing through it. I will persist with the trial and error method of installing things until I am completely baffled, and while my engineering background means I typically have little trouble, there have been times when my wife came to my rescue when I was facing a less intuitive conundrum. The truly marvelous thing is that we work so well together. If we solely followed my method, we'd get to an impasse and stay there for hours trying crazy things. If we just did her process, we'd be reading trivial bits for hours and never get started. Together we get the technology up and running most efficiently.

While gloriously efficient when setting up technology, this difference can have a profoundly detrimental impact on relationships when the couple doesn't understand each other's motivations. When a woman shares a problem, she sees it as a way of bonding with the other person. When a man shares a problem, he is searching for advice—looking for a plan of action. Thus, if a woman shares a difficulty with a man, he will almost always offer advice, even if his advice is shallow and obvious. The woman often then gets upset, thinking the man is belittling her by thinking she didn't already think of his solution. All she wanted was understanding and compassion, not advice. If the problem is particularly difficult, the man will be very uncomfortable because he thinks he is supposed to have an answer. He thus feels less than capable, which might result in the man getting upset and possibly putting down the woman's problem, thinking that if he can minimize her problem he won't have to solve it. Once again, this makes the woman think the guy is less than loving and kind[42].

While women will share their problems with either men or women, men mostly share their problems with other men. This is because men do not wish to lose status by showing a woman their weakness and because they probably have experienced the frustration of sharing something with a woman, and instead of getting good advice all they received was an understanding nod.

Women should note that the underlying desire of men giving advice is probably not to belittle them or to make the men look smarter; instead, they have a sincere desire to help. While people may think chivalry is dead, this is in fact a hard-wired chivalry characteristic. Men want to prove themselves useful to women. Instead of seeing male advice negatively, think of it as a positive since the man is trying to be helpful.

You may also consider that this desire to act is the primary reason your man can be so easily influenced by your flattery. If you want a man to do something, all you have to do is tell him he is good at it or that he is capable when others are not. My wife has me making all the popcorn in the family because she convinced us all that I somehow make it better than she does. There is no rationality to the comment—we both make it the same way—but somehow like Pavlov's dog I persist in always making it, and I feel some kind of strange pride that I do one cooking activity better than she does. You can also convince a man to take out the garbage this way simply by saying it is too heavy for you—almost any complement that makes the man feel special will result in him putting in an extra effort, and almost any nagging will make him much less prone to do the chore.

Let me also offer advice to men (that you can act on!). You will do well to learn to just listen when women talk and not offer advice. If she wants your advice, she will ask for it. If you are like me and simply cannot overcome your biological programming to give (wise?) counsel, it might help if when she finishes telling you her woes you say something like, "That really sounds difficult. I have some ideas on it if you want, but I can sure see that what you are going through is tough." That way she can invite your advice, or you can at least feel you have offered your best whether or not she takes it.

Perhaps the primary brain difference between sexes is the size and activity of the corpus callosum, which acts as a kind of information highway connecting the left and right hemispheres of the brain. For women, the corpus callosum is larger and more bulbous and fires 50% faster than for men[43]. Women are thus better at multitasking and think in a less compartmentalized fashion[44]. Brain imaging reveals that even when men and women perform the same tasks equally well, they typically draw on different parts of the brain to do so; men focus on one part of their brain while women solve problems by integrating areas across the whole brain[45].

This may also be why women typically outperform men in language and memory tests. Men actually house most of their language functions in the left hemisphere and use the left hemisphere about 70-80% of the time, which has the benefit of making them better at tasks that require extended focus. Of course, this also means that women are the only gender continually "in their right minds." To use a sports metaphor, men are often way out in "left field."

Since men tend to use the left hemisphere much more than women, it might be useful to briefly review the different tasks assigned to each hemisphere. It's interesting to note that while the skull is largely symmetrical, the brain is not, having specialized hemispheres with different areas emphasized in each hemisphere. Until recently, scientists made generalizations stating that the left brain is logical and the right is creative, but this distinction requires significant nuance to be understood accurately. In general, the left brain is used when you must be precise or focus on details (such as tool manipulation or using denotative language), when you want to decontextualize a concept so that it can become more clear (such as maps), and when you deal with the general nature of things (categories). It works on issues that are fixed, isolated, and static, and it cuts out or ignores anything it considers irrelevant to the problem at hand.

The right brain, in contrast, deals with awareness of the real world that is full of ambiguity and is constantly exercising a broad vigilance, looking for new things that may be completely irrelevant to the task at hand. It considers things in their native context, is used to interpret metaphor and creativity, and pays attention to body language. The right brain doesn't treat things as abstract concepts but individualizes them and then makes connections to them. It attempts to understand (but not comprehend) what is changing, evolving, interconnected, implicit, and incarnate.

The two hemispheres work in tandem to garner knowledge of the parts (left brain) and put them together to derive wisdom of the whole (right brain). People who are very creative or very logical must use both hemispheres well. Einstein once commented that the intuitive mind is a faithful gift while the rational mind is a faithful servant. Modernism elevated the left brain over the right, honoring the servant but forgetting the gift, whereas postmodernism is in a way a reaction that insists on the ascendency of the right brain in order to rebalance our appreciation of these two hemispheres.[46]

I believe the hemispheric differences and faster-firing corpus callosum in women are also responsible for much of the job specialization that we see. Women are great at multitasking, including the ability to talk on the phone and pay attention to someone talking to them in person at the same time. If you try to talk to most men while they are on the phone, they will quickly get befuddled and possibly upset, since they're only able to concentrate on one conversation at a time. Because men can get so focused, they are often guilty of more obsessive attitudes and can get very "one-track minded." This certainly has some detrimental qualities, but it may lead to superior performance on focus-intensive tasks (like math), and may also be the reason men are at the top of nearly every profession—including traditionally female-dominated occupations like cooking. Interestingly, there are more male geniuses in the world, but there are also more men with sub-average intelligence than women. While upper-level management is dominated by men, there are now more women in the U.S. workforce than men and more women in managerial positions than men.

Since the proverbial train has already "left the station" with regards to comments on traditional roles, let me plunge onward and say that because of their corpus callosum women are probably much better at certain aspects of child-rearing than men. I am fascinated to observe that they have almost a 360-degree radar when watching kids, and can somehow chat with a friend while attentively watching multiple children. When I get to watch the kids, I have to continuously find where they are individually then repeat the process. Like most men, after doing so four or five times I lose interest and become guilty of not paying enough attention to them—I am more in their midst than actually watching them.

Due to brain differences women are also much more attuned to emotional conditions, which can benefit more than just child-raising. Women have larger orbital frontal cortices than men, resulting in differences in emotional perception, experience, and expression[47]. The female brain is considered better at receiving, experiencing and recalling emotional experiences, and because they have a larger mirror-neuron system, women pick up on emotional cues and are much better at interpreting nonverbal emotional cues, facial expressions, body language and in general "reading" another person's emotional state.

This may also be a biological reason for why women consistently show higher levels of empathy because they are better at not only reading another person's emotions but they also are better at feeling the other person's emotions. Perhaps this helps them to be more concerned for others and be better at comforting and nurturing. It furthermore helps women negotiate arguments with each other, though the lack of this ability frustrates women when dealing with men.

Typically in an argument men will attempt to "go neutral" with emotions and look at the issue more objectively, whereas women go the extra mile and try to put themselves in the other person's shoes. The comical part is that the reason men "go neutral" is to attempt to help the situation by getting rid of their emotional bias, but they frustrate women since they come across as both insincere and emotionally detached. When dealing with women, men should attempt to actually see things from the other person's perspective, and women should realize that men are not as adept at this kind of reasoning and "cut them some slack" for at least trying to be less biased in arguments.

Women also benefit from brain differences in a region governing social interaction. One study[48] found that the straight gyrus (a subdivision of the ventral prefrontal cortex) is proportionally 10% larger in women, and its size is directly correlated with a widely-used test of social cognition. Adults who scored higher in interpersonal awareness (thus making them better nurturers) also had larger straight gyruses.

The male brain, however, tends to have a larger dorsal premammillary nucleus, which is the part of the brain governing territorial protection. Coupled with having a larger amygdale, which is the alarm system for threats, men are wired to more readily sense threats and dangers and want to protect their possessions and families. This may also explain the findings that men tend to feel more threatened when their women talk to other men and feel stronger about sexual infidelity than women[49]. Men also have a stronger "flight or fight" reflex to stress, whereas a more feminine strategy is "tend and befriend" (take care of themselves and their children and form stronger social bonds to meet challenges).

Few people will be surprised that men have 2.5 times more brain space devoted to sex, including the interstitial nucleus of the anterior hypothalamus, making this subject a bigger issue for them (and a constant thought that needs to be taken captive and made obedient to Christ, as per II Cor 10:5). Indeed, some studies suggest that men are so concerned about sex that when they are simply told that a woman is observing them, their cognitive ability is impaired[50]. No similar finding was observed in women who were told they were being observed by men.

Even at rest, imaging reveals that male and female brains differ both biologically and cognitively[51]. This may be the biological evidence that supports the common wisdom that men can actually place their minds on idle whereas women are seldom truly just "thinking about nothing." It is comical to observe a woman trying to guess what the man is thinking, not realizing he has the capability to think about nothing. He even has the ability to not care about things she thinks are important and the ability to forget important things without meaning to do so. Indeed, when women try to press these men to reveal their thoughts, the confession that he wasn't really thinking about anything often just serves to make her more suspicious.

Men are also guilty of staying in their "think about nothing" box too long when women want to talk to them. Realizing they will be in trouble if they do not respond, a man will often frantically play back his mental recorder to grasp the last 10 seconds of what the woman was saying so he can pretend he was listening. It takes extra energy for men to switch tasks, so men are reluctant to do so. The biological explanation for this common phenomenon is that because men process so much on in their left hemisphere, they find it more difficult to switch subjects (even from no subject), whereas women can easily switch their attention to something new. Men find switching mental gears slightly bothersome. For example, even when my wife kindly starts a conversation during a commercial break, I find it takes effort to allow myself to be interrupted from watching TV and start paying attention to her.

Finally, women have a proportionately larger deep limbic system, which means they are better tuned in to their own emotions. Coupled with the fact that when they experience pain their left amygdale is activated, whereas when men feel pain their right amygdale is most activated, women are typically more aware of pain, feel it more acutely and constantly, and even require more drugs to mute it. Women will seek treatment for the same pain level far sooner than men, and often women must cajole their men into making a doctor's appointment since men can tune pain out and learn to "just live with it." This brain difference may also be why women are more prone to emotional excesses such as depressions, though, of course, experience and personality play a much greater role here than brain differences.

Genetics also come into the picture, though more research is needed to better understand exactly how they affect behavior. In the past, scientists thought that women pretty much only needed a single X chromosome and that the second X was mostly dormant. Recent studies have shown that certain genes on the second X chromosome escape inactivity. While the Y chromosome gives men several genes that are absent in women, the additional genetic information from the second X chromosome means that about 15 percent of those genes are expressed at higher levels in women. While the exact implications of this finding are still being explored, it gives biological reason to believe that there is much more variability among females than scientists previously thought[52].

Many of the above differences can be detected in academic performance. While men are typically better at holding extended focus and using numbers, women are typically better at language and communication. Interestingly, even though women hold the majority of higher education degrees since 1982, they don't perform as well on standardized tests used for college entrance, possibly due to the intense focus these exams require. While women often outperform men on language processing tasks and draw on more symmetric activation across brain hemispheres, men typically outperform women in tasks that involve activation of the visual cortex areas (spatial reasoning skills)[53].

Studying the brain has also revealed a commonality between men and women that offers more insight into what exactly romantic love is and isn't. Anthropologist and brain expert Helen Fisher[54] has found in multiple studies that when people are in romantic love (not just seeking sex or just attracted to each other), it activates a very primitive and fundamental area of the brain that deals with drives. This means real love is more basic than emotion, reinforcing my earlier contention that love is not an emotion but an act of the will. Love is a basic drive, as strong as the craving for salt and sugar or the need for self-preservation. This is why people are willing to die for love: it actually is placed in the foundation of our brains and can take precedence over all else. This also means love can have addictive properties, including obsession, tolerance building (you just want more), withdrawals when it is removed, and even relapse (a song can bring back the flood of feelings for a lost loved one).

While many long suspected it, only recently have we conclusively identified a biological link between love and sex. It turns out that having orgasm releases a flood of chemicals in the brain, to include dopamine which often results in feelings of attachment[55]. This was created so that married people would stay together more easily, helping them bond in a relationship that lasts a lifetime and creates a stable environment in which to raise children. However, when people have sex outside of marriage, they often experience the chemical bonding but refuse to stay committed and therefore feel intense pain and loneliness with the relationship dissolves. Other couples feel shocked to discover they have attachment when all they wanted was casual sex.

Having multiple sexual partners also poses a problem for the brain, since it eventually learns the pattern of connecting and breaking up, and decides to protect itself by not connecting as completely. This robs people of having the sense of peace and attachment they were meant to enjoy in marriage. Furthermore, in a society that would rather prescribe drugs than deal with underlying issues, far too many people taking antidepressants are unable to form lasting bonds. Many antidepressants include the brain chemical serotonin, which inhibits dopamine receptors and therefore prohibits proper chemical attachment.

The brain's production of dopamine can also explain why people like taking dates to scary movies or on scary rides at the fair. It turns out that arousal and experiencing new things can stimulate dopamine production, and possibly create a sense of attraction.

Fisher tells a story of a graduate student who decided to use this knowledge to his advantage[56]. While visiting Beijing he invited a young lady he liked to go on a rickshaw ride with him. She had never paid him any attention, and so he hoped the thrill of the ride might jump-start some attraction and a relationship. The ride proved to be quite the experience, with images of beautiful Beijing mingling with life-threatening traffic and scintillating turns and twists down narrow streets. When the ride was over the young lady gushed about how exciting it was. The graduate student could see she was excited and somehow turned-on by the ride. He thought maybe the invitation had worked as planned until the lady said, "That was so exciting! And wasn't our rickshaw driver handsome!" Sometimes even the best plans based on the latest scientific knowledge can go awry.

Of course, Adam and Eve didn't have access to any scientific information. In fact, much of it has only come to light in the last few decades, and there is a good chance that much more will come to light in the near future as we rapidly advance in the biosciences. More and more information seems to suggest that men and women are not the same but operate best together and that following God's commands is the best way to behave in conjunction with our biology rather than in opposition to it.

While Adam and Eve and most subsequent generations didn't have the more precise understanding of our biological differences, they did have centuries of trial and error to figure out how to get along. One skill that was developed in the ensuing years is the art of romance, though it seems to be rapidly dying in our reprobate age that overemphasizes sexuality and selfishness. Real romance is not about seduction (though it can lead there in marriage) but is instead about communicating love in a unique and powerful way. In the next chapter we'll look at the phenomenon of romance and discuss how best to communicate love to your partner.

CHAPTER SEVEN FURTHER LEARNING

1) What are some of the issues discussed in this chapter that you have encountered in your relationships?

2) Do you have any extreme forms of your own gender's communication habits that might make it particularly difficult for the other sex to communicate with you? (Hint: if you don't think so, dare to ask your partner about yourself)

3) What was the biggest revelation about your own or your partner's gender that you got from this chapter?

4) Does knowing the differences make a difference? What will YOU do to put this knowledge to good use?

5) What traits typical of your gender are not characteristic of you personally?

CHAPTER 8

Flowers, Figs or Fur Coats: How to be Romantic and Communicate Love

"Women wish to be loved not because they are pretty, or good, or well bred, or graceful, or intelligent, but because they are themselves."
— *Henri Frederic Amiel*

Was Adam romantic in the Garden of Eden? Did sharing a rib slake Eve's need for presents, or did Adam go around the garden picking flowers and offering them as tokens of his love for Eve? Of course we don't have any information on the subject, but at first blush I'd have to say anyone would appear romantic in a beautiful garden where nature serves you perfectly and even the animals want to socialize (or at least be named). What we can be fairly certain about is that Adam and

Eve were truly in love, and they seem to have enjoyed a strong bond because even being kicked out of the garden and cursed with work and pain did not break up their relationship.

Romance is a strange subject to contemplate because it is such a nebulous concept and an abused activity. While I'm not generally a fan of Woody Allen, he may have been on to something when he said, "Men learn to love the woman they are attracted to. Women learn to become attracted to the man they fall in love with[57]." The funny thing is both men and women would have said their initial experience was romantic. For some women romance has been elevated to impossible levels that will prevent them from appreciating the subtler real world of romance, and for some guys romance has been so degraded that they see it merely as a tool to get ladies into bed.

For me, romance is about communicating love is a special way with a loved one, and indeed stress must be placed on "special" as uniqueness is an essential ingredient. Romance inherently conveys a sense of loving in a way that excludes others. That is why you might do a romantic thing with one person then will not repeat it with the next paramour even though it "worked" so well the first time: you see the romantic activity as being reserved for that special person. Indeed, science even agrees that in stark contrast to the "sex drive," people who report being deeply in romantic love have activated particular parts of their brains that involve intense attention, even addiction, to just one other person.[58] This is why discovering the person you are dating has wandering eyes should give you a clue that you are not as special to them as you ought to be in an intimate relationship.

While the Bible contains romantic sentiments, the concept was not developed in ancient times, and the word never appears in the Bible. We do see romance being played out, for example, in the Songs of Solomon and even between our God and the Church, but overall the Bible is less of a resource on romance than it is on its fundamental theme of love. I am unfortunately furthermore challenged by this subject because I am a man, and it seems that while women have a natural grasp of what is romantic, men must fumble through and learn the art with little inherent skill. This also explains why most of this chapter will speak to men in an effort to make them understand how to be romantic, and only at the end of the chapter will we broach the subject of how to romance a man.

On the plus side, I have discovered that in this subject more experiential learning is better than taking an academic approach and that to be romantic involves a spontaneity that is often destroyed by academic research. A big key to the whole subject is simply being willing to be out of your mind for the other person, and the more you act on this "craziness" the more romantic your actions will be. Thus this section has less science, but it may in the end include more wisdom. Our goal is to learn how to communicate our romantic love in ways that are best received by our paramours.

The first lesson to learn about romance is that it is paradoxical and doesn't make sense. If it made logical sense men would probably be better at it, but instead it is more intuitive, and thus women specialize in it. Many women go so far as to think there is some kind of force in the universe that generates love and ensures the "right" couples get together and fall in love. Often this entity in romantic movies goes by the name "fate" or "serendipity" or "cosmic force," but in the final analysis all these words are merely substitutes for our awesome God whom the Hollywood writers wish to reject. Thus people in these movies just bump into each other repeatedly against all odds and eventually feel attracted to each other because the universe seems to want them to be together.

Let's be clear: there is no universal force that is pulling people together in love if there is no God. Furthermore, without God nothing we do has any meaning anyway. It is astonishing to see our generation rejecting God but searching for meaning. Our lives have no permanence or real meaning unless they are placed into the context of God and His will. But once we have God in the picture, we most certainly can believe in miracles and look for His hand guiding circumstance and even moving us to meet and fall in love. One could even say God is what makes the world romantic. He certainly is the One who gives life meaning.

Planned spontaneity

Whether or not they believe in God, I have found that most women relate spontaneity and serendipity with romance. They like the idea that they are being pushed by an unknown force into a relationship—that it is their destiny to be engaged to the man of their dreams. They have been trained to expect a perfect relationship from a perfect man, and that all circumstances will funnel them into a deeper love for their future husband. Maybe it was indeed this way in the Garden of Eden. There all nature must have worshiped God and respected humanity and must have worked together to increase Adam and Eve's bliss.

Men know Eden is gone, and idealistic sentimentality does not make for a great way to plan a date (or wait to get one!). In the real world you have to act to create your own destiny. You must act to overcome things that go wrong, or women who misunderstand your intentions might want "to just be friends." Sometimes you even must act just to ensure the eligible lady who consumes your attention recognizes your existence. A man must be clever and act if he is to meet and woo the woman of his dreams.

However, careful planning and hard work to get to know someone isn't romantic. In fact, it is downright mundane, and women can't even deceive themselves into feeling that fate has drawn them into a relationship when the guy obviously manipulated events in order to get her attention. Thus the conundrum is that women want things to "just happen," and men know that things don't "just happen" on their own. That is why I have developed what I call "planned spontaneity."

Perhaps the story of how I got engaged will best explain the principle and showcase it in action. As described earlier, I knew it was God's will that I marry Rebecca the first time I saw her, and after two months God also revealed His will to Rebecca that she should marry me. When I was told my response was something like: "OK, I'll work on that and make it happen," whereas my wife's response to God was: "Prove it." Still, within a few months we were both soundly in love and had no doubts about where we were heading. I was thus faced with the problem of making our engagement proposal special and somewhat of a surprise when we already both knew we would one day marry.

I'll discuss some more details of the engagement process in chapter 10, but suffice it to say that I took leave of work and without telling her I asked her parents if I had their permission to propose. I also made a lot of arrangements then asked if she wanted to drive three hours over the Cascade mountains, stopping to explore some caves on the way, and spend Labor Day weekend with my family in Yakima, Washington.

On that trip we discussed many things, and I shared with her how I had been thinking of marriage and basically tried to feel her out on the subject. I discovered what I already knew: she was comfortable with the concept and was somewhat expecting it to happen sometime. I therefore asked her if it would be all right with her if we went on a series of expensive dates, and on one of them I would propose. I told her I didn't want her to feel let down when I didn't propose after a nice date but that instead we would make it into a kind of game, and she would have to endure so that it would be a surprise. It did not surprise me when she agreed to go on a series of expensive dates with me, since I was going to pay for them.

Being the clever man that I am, I calculated that the most surprise would come by proposing on the first expensive date because that would be when she was least expecting it. That would save me money, too! Okay, maybe I'm more frugal than clever, and rationalizing to be cheap is NOT romantic thinking (as if there were such a thing!), but it was still a helpful determining factor, and I needed to save money to pay for the ring I already had in my pocket.

In fact, while I had planned a nice outing at the weekend's conclusion, my thinking was that if the cave exploration or any other event that weekend presented a good opportunity, I'd be ready for it. I had planned fun events but was ready to be struck by the moment. While the caves were fun and even a bit romantic, we left them behind still unengaged. Fortunately, I also still had the ring in my pocket—I was worried about losing it while I was crawling about in the caves.

At my parents' house I told them of my plans to get engaged and received their blessing. We had a nice time there, and then my plan swung into effect. On Sunday night Rebecca's mother Judy called and told her that our Monday plan to visit Rebecca's family could not happen because her aunt was sick. I had arranged with Judy to make this call, and I had even given her a line she could use to skirt lying yet still deceive Rebecca, but her mother fell into the roll with gusto. When Rebecca told me about the call, I was surprised her mother had made it sound so serious. Instead of just being freed from going to the party, Rebecca was a bit upset and worried about her sick relative.

I consoled Rebecca and told her we'd have fun anyway and that we'd take this opportunity to go on our first expensive date. She wanted to know the details, but all I said was that she needed to wear a nice dress. Though it is important not to tell the woman where you are going or what you are doing since that makes it seem more spontaneous, it is still wise to instruct the lady on what to wear so that she is comfortable on your date. I'm sure Rebecca thought I wasn't telling her about the date because I didn't know myself, and since we stayed up late playing board games with the family Sunday night, she certainly wasn't expecting me to have made extensive plans for our Monday excursion.

On Monday we enjoyed my family a bit more then drove the two hours to Seattle, arriving at the base of the Seattle Space Needle in time for an early dinner. Surprisingly (for Rebecca), we had reservations, and we received nice window seats that overlooked the city and revolved one full time every hour. We enjoyed our meal, but I don't remember the conversation much. Most of what I remember was thinking about when would be the best time to ask the big question. While I knew the night was young and other plans would come into play, my palms were sweaty, and I had to be very careful not to give away my excitement.

About half way through the filet minion, a man showed up with a dozen roses and tried to hand them to Rebecca. Thinking that the cost would be added to our dinner bill, she politely declined, only to discover that the man would not take no for an answer and soon had thrust the dozen red roses along with a two page poem into her hands before quickly leaving. A bit startled, she soon realized the delivery of roses and poem had been prearranged. In fact, the poem had been written by me and was all about our experiences together, in part focusing on our love of high places.

To clarify, a month after we started to see each other I was required by the military to attend the Defense Information School in Fort Meade, Maryland. After two months of being apart I flew Rebecca to the East Coast to attend my graduation, and then we explored New York City together.

Our first kiss was on top of the Empire State Building. Ever since that event we make sure that we kiss on every high place, which was great fun when we explored castles in England and Italy. I highly (pun intended) encourage making a tradition of kissing, whether it is when you pass over state borders, when you are on water, or for any other excuse. While I feel our tradition of high places is fun, after 16 years of marriage I realize it could have been even better—I should have chosen ground floors so that I got more kisses.

After the dinner we went up the stairs to the top of the Seattle Space Needle and out into the open air, similar to the Empire State Building. Few people were around, so we enjoyed the warm evening complete with sunset, and, of course, we enjoyed our traditional kiss. After that I led Rebecca back down the tower. I'm certain that she felt that if I were going to ask her to marry me, that would have been a great place. Still, she was consoled knowing that she could look forward to more fun dates.

As we pulled out of the city I pretended to make a wrong turn and headed north instead of south, something that is fairly easy to do with all the one-way streets in Seattle. Rebecca patiently told me I was heading the wrong way and wondered why I didn't drive more aggressively to get off the interstate highway as soon as possible. A few exits away I did get off but once again seemed to make a mistake and missed the on-ramp going south. Used to giving me directions, Rebecca decided to take charge and tell me how to get back to the highway. However, she then recognized where we were and asked if I would be interested in extending the evening by going to a neat spot that had docks and a beach. Since that was exactly where I was trying to get, I let her direct me to this special beach and even took a wrong turn or two when she directed me to do so because I wanted to keep up the ruse that this was all her idea.

We pulled into the small parking lot, got out of the car, and had a romantic walk along the docks. The city sprawled across the bay, with lovely lights piercing the darkness and even providing a kind of ambiance lighting since a soft glow was created from the lights being reflected off the clouds; there are almost always clouds in Seattle. When we reached the end of the docks, we decided to take off our shoes, roll up my pants and her dress to knee height, and wade into the Puget Sound. The water was a bit cold but seemed pleasant since the evening was warm. While silence is often romantic, it is not really my style, so I kept trying to ensure we engaged in deep discussion and pushed the conversation toward important things of self-revelation.

As we exited the water, Rebecca revealed that she didn't want to spend her life alone, so I told her I could do something about that and got down on one knee in the sand and began my proposal speech. It was a good one. I had spent months writing and memorizing it, but when I delivered it, I forgot it was memorized and just spoke from my heart. I'll spare you the details, but I will say I told her that while I couldn't promise her monetary riches, she would always be rich with love, that I could not promise her everything she'd always wanted, but I would always keep life interesting, and that if she married me, I would be faithful and treat her as God's daughter deserves to be treated. I said I would lead her where God leads our family and that I would serve her as Christ served the church. But enough oratory. I concluded with the famous words: "Will you marry me?" and offered her a diamond ring.

Interestingly, she didn't answer. I guess she couldn't. She just grabbed me and hugged me. After a minute or two I pushed away a bit and asked, "So does that mean you'll marry me?" That is when she finally confirmed it. I then tried to direct her to walking further down the beach, but she said she couldn't walk and just wanted to sit down. I told her we'd walk another 20 or 30 feet to find a nice place, and when she persisted in trying to sit there on the spot, I told her if she didn't walk I'd carry her.

We thus went a little further down the beach arm in arm and quickly arrived at a fairly secluded spot near the woods that came up to the beach. There was a blanket on the sand surrounded by lit candles and Hershey's kisses sprinkled around. In a silver bowl was ice and a bottle of sparkling apple cider, along with a chilled wine glass. There was even a radio that had a cassette tape continuously playing our song softly in the background. It certainly appeared that the universe had conspired to give us a perfect night and ensure we would be a couple forever.

Okay, so the universe had little to do with it. While Rebecca stumbled from one seemingly spontaneous event to the next, I, of course, had it all planned out. My brother David and his wife Rosie lived in Seattle, and they had ensured the roses and poem were delivered and had set up our romantic night picnic spot. While I am not necessarily an expert on romance, I am assured by every woman I tell this story to that I did a good job. For me, it was weeks of planning, but for my wife it was all seemingly spontaneous. That is planned spontaneity. That is romantic.

I should add here that we spent a few hours just enjoying the view and talking about our future together. When you get engaged, be sure to plan in time for your wife-to-be to tell you all about what she wants for the wedding, what dates will work, and all the other details. I can't say I listened very well to that conversation—I just basked in the knowledge that I would spend the rest of my life with the woman of my dreams. That's not quite right. She was even better than my dreams.

Unconditional Love and Conditional Respect

The Bible contains a lot of wisdom on loving relationships, but almost all of its advice is given for marital relationships. Thus while we can learn a lot from its instruction, we must realize that dating/courting is not the same as marriage. We will therefore look at the Bible's wisdom and try to contextualize it for a dating/courting relationship.

Most people are familiar with the Bible's brilliant insight into the needs of men and women, so I will be fairly brief on the obvious and extrapolate the less discussed details. Probably the most quoted passage on what to do in marriage is Ephesians 5:21-33 that says:

"Submit to one another out of reverence for Christ. Wives, submit to your husbands as to the Lord. For the husband is the head of the wife as Christ is the head of the church, his body, of which he is the Savior. Now as the church submits to Christ, so also wives should submit to their husbands in everything. Husbands, love your wives, just as Christ loved the church and gave himself up for her to make her holy, cleansing her by the washing with water through the word, and to present her to himself as a radiant church, without stain or wrinkle or any other blemish, but holy and blameless. In this same way, husbands ought to love their wives as their own bodies. He who loves his wife loves himself. After all, no one ever hated his own body, but he feeds and cares for it, just as Christ does the church—for we are members of his body. 'For this reason a man will leave his father and mother and be united to his wife, and the two will become one flesh.' This is a profound mystery— but I am talking about Christ and the church. However, each one of you also must love his wife as he loves himself, and the wife must respect her husband." (NIV)

It is vital that we realize the first part of the instruction clearly admonishes both partners in a marriage to submit to each other. This essential advice dwarfs the rest of the passage, and failure to submit to each other is why many marriages fail—especially marriages between two first born children which are often fraught with conflict. To be a Christian means to have died to one's self and now live for Christ: you trade your life today for the perfect life Jesus lived 2000 years ago.

This means that we strive to make choices like we believe Jesus would, and we surrender all of our "rights" to God. Our society is so rights-conscious that it is often hard to pull away and simply let God rule. If we are fully surrendered to God, we will be able to submit to each other, as we follow Jesus' example who, "…being in very nature God, did not consider equality with God something to be grasped, [7] but made himself nothing, taking the very nature of a servant, being made in human likeness. [8] And being found in appearance as a man, he humbled himself and became obedient to death— even death on a cross!" (Philippians 2:6-8, NIV).

Both partners in a marriage submit to each other, and both partners in a dating relationship must also start learning how to submit. Submission before marriage is, of course, more limited, but warning bells should ring if it feels like only one person is submitting, and the other is always getting his or her way. Even while courting it is important that the relationship involve mutual submission.

The real genius of the Ephesians 5 passage is its admonishment for wives to respect their husbands whereas husbands are to love their wives. In keeping with our context of pre-marriage relationships I'll not go into too much depth, but it is vital that we recognize men and women have different needs and will feel loved in different ways. What is most often overlooked is that while women need unconditional love, men need conditional respect.

Women really crave unconditional love. While they spend inordinate amounts of time trying to deserve attention by working on their physical appearance or some skill, when all is said and done what they really want is to be loved for who they are. Just like the quote at the beginning of this chapter says, women want to be loved for being themselves, not for their appearance or actions. They want completely undeserved love. Men make a huge mistake when they link their love for a woman to performance. Men will often say "I love you" in the same breath as "You are a great cook," and a woman hears, "I am loved because I cook" rather than the intended distinction between the comments.

My wife used to ask me "Why?" after I told her how great I thought she was, or after I said I loved her. I foolishly would then try to quantify all the things I liked about her thinking this would make her even happier. In truth, it had a dampening effect on my initial statement of love. Eventually I learned that the correct answer was to simply reply, "Because I love you" with no description for why that fact exists. Rebecca needed to know that I loved *her*, not her beauty or actions or how I felt when I was around her.

Giving unconditional love is difficult for men since what they most require is conditional respect. They thus keep trying to justify or give conditions for their love and often thwart their own intentions. As discussed in chapter one, I believe Adam was made in God's image in multiple ways, and one of those ways was his ability to generate love. Adam, like God, had so much love that he needed someone to give his love to. Eve was made to complement this ability, so women crave a man's love that is generated by his choice rather than a love that is compelled by appearance or actions. Real men can choose to give love for absolutely no reason whatsoever.

On the other hand, women make an opposite mistake when they try to give men respect for no reason at all. It is little use to tell a man "I respect you" if you can't tell him why. Men want to know what it is they are doing that is correct so they can do more of it and make it part of their character. Perhaps this springs from childhood or simply begins in childhood, as boys constantly want their mother's praise and will go to great lengths to have their mothers approve their drawings or Lego creations. Men want to be respected for a reason and will discount unsubstantiated statements of respect.

To be very practical, this means women must look for the things they like about their man and let him know about them. If you liked the way he took defeat with grace, tell him so. If you respect his efforts digging a ditch, tell him how you admire his efforts. Wherever you see something in a man that is admirable, you would show him respect by letting him know of your admiration. My bet is that your man will not only feel respected but also will work extra hard to improve even in the areas where he is already doing well.

On the other hand, a guy should avoid telling a woman he loves her in a sentence with other compliments. Instead, he should look at his woman and contemplate how much he loves her. He should shun thoughts of how beautiful she is or how smart she is or how she does the right things and should instead simply dwell on his love for her. When he feels the love for her in the depth of his being, that is the perfect time to tell her he loves her. My bet is that she'll feel the sincerity of the words, and he will understand that any qualification or condition to the love would only mitigate its power.

Beyond the biblical truth that woman need love and men need respect, it also seems true that people have their own "love language." Gary Chapman's *The Five Love Languages*[59] describes this concept well. The book's central truth is that people express love differently and that typically the way a person expresses love is how they wish to be loved. This means that if we want to love someone well, we need to express our love in their "love language." The five love languages Chapman identifies are gift giving, spending quality time together, verbal praise, performing acts of service, and giving physical touch. Most of us want to give love in the method we most wish to receive it, but to truly choose to love means to express love in the recipient's love language. We'd all do well to understand our partner's love language and try to "speak" it fluently.

At the same time, I think we need to be multilingual when it comes to love. While we need to understand our partner's love language, we should try to at least occasionally express our love in all five love languages. The more time and effort and creativity you put into communicating love the more personal and thus romantic it will be. Just as God tells us He loves us in everything from the Spirit's still small voice to creation's glory to Jesus' dwelling among us, so we must express our love in multifarious ways. Learning these "languages" may be difficult, but they are worth the effort when you look into your loved one's eyes and see they understand your heart.

Romantic Gifts: Flowers, Figs, or Furs

Randy Pausch in his best-selling *The Last Lecture*[60] wrote,

"It took a long time, but I've finally figured it out. When it comes to men who are romantically interested in you, it's really simple. Just ignore everything they say and only pay attention to what they do." While "actions speak louder than words" in our media-saturated culture full of emails and text messages, actions are often drowned out by words. Gift giving is one way to give this trend pause and clearly communicate love.

There is no doubt that gift giving is one of the love languages that holds an important place in communicating love early in a relationship. Giving gifts allows you to sacrifice for your loved one, symbolize your love through an icon that will endure, or simply show that you thought a lot about the other person because you gave them the exact thing they most wanted.

Our culture has largely eviscerated the loving act of gift giving by making it a mass experience complete with entire grocery store aisles full of identical-looking hearts and candies. It also has sadly turned much of gift giving into an obligation that is met by finding a "great deal" rather than being an act of love that overflows from the heart and seeks to discover the "perfect something" to make the recipient happy.

Your goal in gift giving must be to shirk the commercialization and instead concentrate on discovering what will be treasured by the one you love. I have seen people with the spiritual gift of giving always deliver the exact thing that warms the heart most and says "you're loved" at the right time. I have also seen men who are simply baffled by the entire idea of giving a gift, they capitulate to culture and spend a lot on something with little meaning (or worse yet, go to a store and ask the clerk what they should buy!)

Here is a quick test to see if you naturally know what is most romantic. What should Adam have given Eve in the Garden of Eden: flowers, figs, or a fur coat? Flowers symbolize things that are beautiful but evanescent, figs are a type of food and thus very practical and useful, while fur coats in Eden suggest something that is expensive but that his loved one had never asked for. I am, of course, assuming this is happening before the Fall—after the Fall the fur coat must have been more necessary since God had fur garments made for both Adam and Eve.

The romantic choice is the flowers, but what is enlightening is the reason flowers trump the figs and fur coat. I realize that different women want different things, and even the same woman is often not entirely consistent about what she wants, but overall women want gifts that cost something (in time or money) but have little intrinsic value. This is because such gifts send the message that the woman is special and that the real reason the gift is being given has nothing to do with the gift itself being wonderful but is purely because the woman is wonderful.

The more practical the gift, the more the gift receives glory instead of the woman. Figs are a bad choice because they are good to eat, and maybe the man bought them hoping she would share. Even giving a gift just because it is expensive (like the fur coat) is a mistake. If there is value in the object, it may be because the object is great that it was purchased rather than because the woman recipient is great. Meaningless expensive gifts should be avoided; if an expensive gift is given, it must say something about the relationship or at least communicate that the man knew exactly what the lady wanted rather than just having the merit of being expensive.

Some might object and say that women like expensive jewelry precisely because it is expensive. I agree jewelry is a special case, but it still follows the overall pattern I have outlined. Consider that at its core jewelry is basically overworked lumps of rock and metal, and the only reason it costs so much is that women like it. I'm convinced that if the world were made up of all men, the gold and diamond markets would collapse, and there would be few if any jewelry stores in malls (Of course, there may also be no malls). Jewelry is an expensive thing that should be worthless but is not. I would further add that women do not just like jewelry because it is expensive; they also like it because it is associated with fidelity. Rings are the near-universal symbol of marriage, so they are tokens of enduring love. The high price of most jewelry also means that buying it makes a significant investment which shows a woman that her man is willing to sacrifice for her happiness.

Giving your lady friend jewelry (not costume jewelry which says your love is as fake as the plastic rocks) also has the added benefit of allowing her to show her friends how much you love her. It reminds her of your love throughout the day, because every flash of light off the gold says, "Look, someone loves me!" If you have given her copious amounts of jewelry it has the added bonus of serving as an early warning system for you—when she's not wearing your gifts you may want to see if everything is okay in the relationship.

Your goal must be to get something that is extravagant or something that has meaning for your particular relationship. The less practical and the more memory-invoking the better. That is why women like expensive candy that is consumed in a day, flowers that die in a week, or even romantic violin serenades that only linger in memory after the last note is played. In general, make your gifts fleeting, impractical, and filled with meaning from your relationship—in short, make them romantic.

You certainly can also succeed in romance with very little money. Give her a four-leaf clover from the field where you first kissed. This may be inexpensive, but it cost you a lot of time and consideration to find. Call up your lady and play a romantic song like Stevie Wonder's "I just called to say I love you" then hang up. She'll most likely call you back, so turn off your phone—nothing you can say will add to the sentiment. This song is especially appropriate not just because it involves calling but because it is about the whimsy of loving "just because." You can even get a trinket from a shared memory and start a game of hide and seek. Since we got engaged after being on the Seattle Space Needle, I bought a $4 Space Needle key chain, and my wife and I enjoy hiding it in places where the other will find it and feel loved.

If you have no idea what is romantic, and your creativity is failing you, our culture can come to your rescue as a last resort. After all, some items are intrinsically romantic, so even men without a single romantic bone in their bodies can simply put some of these elements together and hope for the best. For example, hearts are romantic. Chocolate is romantic. Small things are often cute and romantic. Put these things together and you have small chocolate hearts—very romantic.

Other cute (and potentially romantic) things include the colors red and pink, teddy bears, kittens, and puppies. Women also often like fancy frills and curly things because romance has to do with flair and flourishes. If you buy her a romantic greeting card, get the one in reds and pinks featuring one of the creatures listed above (or heart shapes) and be sure to put her name on the outside of the envelope using great tails for your g's and y's. Large loops on your b's, d's and p's are also nice, as well as sort of swirly underlining connected to the letters.

An alternative plan is to get the greeting cards that mix black and white with just a touch of color, especially if you wish to convey fidelity. Gift cards featuring two kids who are in black and white and dressed like old people and seem to be sharing a romantic moment with only the rose in color are especially powerful. Such cards conjure images of "classic" and "enduring" as well as purity (youth), spontaneity (since children don't generally plan ahead), and passion (red roses).

Often images from the idealized Middle Ages are also romantic. Think castles, gallant knights, princes, princesses, and the whole notion of chivalry. While attending a Middle Ages reenactment fair risks being distracted by *Harry Potter* and *Lord of the Rings* groupies (definitely not romantic!), watching horses charge in a mock joust and seeing the flags and pageantry may be a great romantic outing. We'll discuss more dating ideas in the next chapter.

The proper use of light can be very romantic. Sunrises and

sunsets are romantic, especially when they paint the sky with the romantic color red. Nearly all candles are romantic, as are the low light levels you see at romantic restaurants. Low light is probably why dinner dates are more romantic than lunch dates. Those restaurants also know that background music is important to evoke romance. Such music must be soft and not distracting; it's often most effective if it is particularly artful (like soft jazz) or originates from a romantic culture (such as Italian music).

With all these things to give, maybe it is best to conclude this section by warning you what to avoid giving. Avoid giving kitchen appliances or anything that is related to work because that suggests to the woman that she is valued only because of her culinary talent or work ability. If cartoons are to be trusted, frying pans are especially to be avoided because they can be used as a club to great effect. Note that if cooking is special to your woman, you can give her kitchen appliances because then the gift says you know who she is and that you put thought into getting her exactly what she wanted. But avoid giving anything that makes the woman feel your love is conditional—your gift needs to say "I love you for who you are, and not for anything that you do."

Romantic Maturity

Since what women are primarily looking for is maturity, being mature also has a romantic dimension. Women prefer gentleness to macho, thoughtfulness to chivalry, loving actions rather than just words. They are far more impressed when you lose with grace than when you win with excessive bravado.

When complemented, deflect the praise rather than basking in it. Whatever you do, avoid being brutish or self-centered as these are antithetical to romance since they are self-focused rather than other-focused.

Many men sabotage their own romantic impulses by acting immature. They set up a romantic event but then feel awkward as they enact it, so they become goofy. I'm not saying humor can never be romantic, but goofiness will pretty much kill the moment. This is because being goofy is acting immature. You never see James Bond getting goofy while wooing a woman. Being romantic is serious business—you are trying to demonstrate and communicate the sincerity of your love. Therefore you must keep a straight face and reject the temptation to sabotage your own romantic endeavors.

Concentrate on creating special memories that are uniquely shared by you and your partner. Create environments of security and intimacy and steer the discussion to deep self-revelation. Few things are as romantic as sharing an inner feeling or a private memory or telling someone exactly how important they are to you.

Of course romance also needs to be tempered by understanding the phase of your relationship. Being mature in relationships means understanding that going too far too fast is a big mistake and can scare the other person away. While I felt God told me the moment I saw Rebecca that she was the one I would marry, I certainly did not immediately confide that knowledge to her. In fact, even weeks later she didn't know I was working behind the scenes to orchestrate our relationship.

Another caution is that if you have been in a relationship

for a long time with no romance, you may need to take it to a higher level or risk your partner doubting the relationship. If you have been together for some time and both feel the Lord is blessing the relationship, there is nothing wrong with occasionally sharing romantic moments wherein you better articulate your love for each other.

As discussed in chapter 2, the best thing you can do to attract a future spouse is to become more like Christ. We do not know how romantic Jesus would have been because clearly His mission didn't include getting married. This is quite powerful when you think about it, since the greatest gift on earth that man receives is woman, and God denied this gift to His own Son. However, my guess is that Jesus would have been quite a romantic since He knew how to communicate love, sometimes with words and other times with actions.

Romancing a Man

This may disappoint women, but in general men do not need romance and simply feel awkward when women try to romance them. In romantic moments a guy knows he is supposed to feel special but instead he mostly feels stupid and wonders if he can conjure the proper reaction to make his woman know he appreciates the sentiment. Indeed, for the most part men associate being romanced with being seduced, and this kind of romance is therefore best left for after marriage (and discussion in another book!)

A woman can, of course, communicate love to a man before marriage, but it will look more like flirting than romance. Guys are impressed when ladies show them special attention or leave little notes expressing love or just wink at them from across the room. Go to his music recital, cheer him on at a sports game, or watch a football game with him and the other guys. Basically, any special attention is good enough for a guy.

When it comes to gifts, don't think romantic but instead think practical. What is his favorite soda or candy bar or drink from the expensive coffee joint? Give him a gift card to Best Buy or his favorite apparel store. Have his favorite type of pizza delivered to his dorm room—trust me, he'll eat it even if he already had dinner.

On the topic of eating, instead of going to the romantic Italian food restaurant on his birthday, take him to a sports motif restaurant like Red Robin or Buffalo Wild Wings. You'll show your love for him far more and spend less if you react to his idea of a good time rather than trying to create a romantic moment.

Planned spontaneity also works on men but for a different reason. While women want to think there is a cosmic force pulling people together, not telling the guy what is going on makes a woman seem more mysterious, which makes her more feminine and alluring. This sentiment is captured in the Disney song *A Whole New World* as the male sings about "a thrilling chase." Most men are like lions who want to play with their game rather than get it easily, and the smart woman will spice up the relationship by taking her guy on adventures without him knowing where she is leading. Men fall in love with women who show themselves to be full of energy and are willing to go out and do things with their man.

I'm convinced that part of what attracts men to women is the feminine mystique: men often are captivated by trying to understand women. Guys wonder why women are not more straight forward, and describe women as being "catty" or coy. While this is often a complaint, it is also precisely what keeps their attention and interest.

I'm sure part of the reason women send conflicting signals is because they are not entirely convinced about the guy in question, but I also think that unconsciously women are testing guys. A lady might use nonverbal cues and speak in circles to see if the guy is willing to expend the effort to understand her. Thus, instead of feeling frustrated, the man should see the woman's coyness as an invitation to prove his interest level by sticking with the conversation and trying to really understand where she is coming from. If the guy gives up, it means he doesn't value the relationship enough or doesn't know her well enough. If he sticks with it, he shows he is willing to put in the effort to know her, and that in itself says, "I love you."

Possibly the best way to end a chapter on romance is to say that you should listen to your loved one. Romance has at its core the purpose of communicating love, and listening communicates interest and a willingness to understand the other person. Listening and observing will help you get to know the other person and discern what is romantic for them.

On the other hand, when someone is putting in the extra effort to be romantic, it is incumbent upon the recipient to listen and be appreciative of the expression. Many people are too scared to allow themselves to be loved. Sometimes it is loving just to accept love.

In the next chapter we will look at some courting/dating ideas that will help you build memories and better get to know your loved one. You may be surprised to discover that the best dates are doing things you don't like to do together and that the most insights may come from being out with other company rather than always being out just as a couple.

CHAPTER EIGHT FURTHER LEARNING

1) On a 1-10 scale, how romantic are you? How about your paramour?
2) On a 1-10 scale, how much do you appreciate romance?
3) What is one way you can improve how you communicate love?
4) What is your love language? What is your paramour's love language?
5) What do you find to be most romantic?
6) What was your most romantic moment? Alternatively, what is your ideal version of romance from a movie?
7) What idea in this chapter did you think was most romantic?
8) What romantic outing can you plan to create a memory, and then what thing can you give that invokes that memory?

CHAPTER 9

Talking in the Garden: Essential Dates and Discussions

"Now Eros makes a man really want, not a woman, but one particular woman. In some mysterious but quite indisputable fashion the lover desires the Beloved herself, not the pleasure she can give. No lover in the world ever sought the embraces of the woman he loved as the result of a calculation, however unconscious, that they would be more pleasurable than those of any other woman." — *C.S. Lewis, The Four Loves*

In Genesis 4:1 the Bible describes sexual union between Adam and Eve using the Hebrew word *yada,* which has at its root "to know." While the euphemism certainly indicates Adam "knew" Eve physically, I think it should be thought of as indicating much more than that. Any two people can sexually touch (and sadly our current "hook-up" culture has far too much of that), but it takes substance and character to "know" another person at a deeper level. Mature people understand that knowing someone deeply not only makes the relationship more satisfying but also makes the sexual relationship more satisfying in marriage. We were designed to know one person intimately, both personally and sexually, and even to unite with them so that the two become "one flesh." This intimate relationship was meant to last a lifetime and is a foretaste of Heaven, where I believe we will know and be known intimately without the need for physical union (see Luke 12:2).

C.S. Lewis' quote at the start of the chapter is very true. Love never happens because we are trying to experience it, but instead develops as we seek to experience a particular person. Getting to know the other person well is not only a joyous journey but is also essential for you to decide if this is the right person to marry. This chapter will help you go much deeper in your relationship, helping you to begin to develop a "soul mate" connection of true intimacy based on really knowing your partner. The key, of course, is to be interested in each other, and to ask good questions and learn to listen well to the answers. Your goal is to understand each other and you will find that in the process you learn about yourself. Try to understand your paramour's motivations, fears, hopes, and "rulebook of life" so that you can see the world through his or her eyes.

I'm not proud of my first date with Rebecca. We went to Pizza Hut, then a movie, then stayed up until early morning talking. The pizza was unremarkable, the movie was forgettable, but the conversation was outstanding. It's funny that the one activity that night that was completely free was absolutely priceless.

Thankfully, I learned a lot about planning dates since that first date with the woman who would eventually become my wife. I like to think I got better at dating as indicated by our engagement date described in chapter 8. There are all kinds of dates, ranging from the best ones that are well-crafted and maximize interaction to those that are more tentative wastes of time in which two people are together but hardly benefit from one another's presence. Having been married for many years I can appreciate the need for dates throughout the spectrum, but when you are just starting a relationship, you only have a limited amount of time together to get to know each other and make the right impression, which means a wise person will plan dates carefully.

While it can be an arduous duty, planning dates can also be fun and certainly can be filled with purpose. Dates can show off your knowledge of the other person's likes or display your creativity or highlight your many connections and relationships in a given area. Some of the most romantic dates involve a lot of careful planning, which tells your date you were thinking about them and that you were willing to invest time and money to please them. Dates can also be carefully crafted to elicit discoveries about each other or to help you know how the other person behaves in less common situations. You can design dates that are centered entirely on the other person or plan activities that please both participants. Rarely should you plan something that only you want to do. In fact, one of my mistakes on that first date was that both pizza and watching a movie are things I like to do, and I failed to take into consideration her preferences.

On the other hand, I was trying to make the experience light-hearted and not get too deep too quickly. Where you are in a relationship should most certainly play an important role in how you plan dates. If you spring a very romantic date on your partner too soon, they may be scared away or just feel awkward throughout the evening. On the other hand, a romantic date may be just the perfect thing to move the relationship forward, showing that you want to not only be friends but also start considering each other for marriage.

Light Dates and Discussions

At the beginning of a relationship you want to put the other person at ease and maximize the ability to interact. In high school I found miniature golf to be perfect, providing an activity as well as plenty of time for conversation. While many women can easily converse for hours doing little else, most men prefer to converse while they are doing something. That is why often the best part of a date is driving between locations, since the guy thinks he is accomplishing something and both people have little else to do than talk. If you anticipate an inability to converse, be sure to have light music on in the background, but if you want to best facilitate conversation, turn off the radio and engage in conversation.

When planning dates realize that men like a plan of action whereas women like options. Thus a woman can plan a date and just tell the man what is happening, and he will be thrilled.

If the man is planning the date, he should consider the principles in chapter 8 and consider hiding events from his date and maybe even giving her options along the way. For instance, he could pick her up, tell her he has planned a "choose your own adventure date," and then throughout the evening give her some limited options for what will take place next.

In the beginning of a relationship something simple and not too costly works best. If the lady likes movies, you can take her to one that is appropriate (make sure you read the reviews before you go!), but be sure to include time after the movie for discussion. Sometimes a movie can be a good launching place for a chat, and your local ice cream place or Panera Bread might be ideal for having an unimposing discussion.

There are many more creative dates than going to the movies. You might try going to the zoo, roller skating or ice skating, or even skiing. While it is nice if you have skills in the area, you might find it even more enjoyable if you both learn something together. Small hikes, horse buggy rides downtown, and amusement parks can all be great ways to impress your date. The most important thing is to plan an event that forces you to be together and allows you to talk. Dates are successful when you get to discover more about each other.

Research suggests that although men and women share a few conversation interests, there are topics the other gender may not be very interested in discussing. Common ground topics include work issues and entertainment interests such as movies, television shows, or music preferences.

Women-specific conversation areas include relationships,

family, health, diets, food, clothes, men, and other women. Ladies are prone to gossip about family and friends and do not stick with exactly what was said or done but will get into analyses of other people's motivations.

Men do not talk about others as much, and when they do it is more confined to discussing actual actions or words rather than attempting to read motivations. Men-specific topics include current events, business, sports, and other men. They gossip more about distant personalities such as media and sports celebrities rather than immediate relationships. They rarely discuss women with each other because if they have something positive to say, it might spark interest and create competition, and if they have something negative to say, it is usually said with a quick off-color label rather than an analysis. In fact, when a guy returns to the dorm room his roommate might ask if she was "hot," and if it was fun, and the conversation ends in a minute or two. This is about 3 hours shorter than the similar conversation happening in the ladies' dorm room.

Note that each gender will complain that the other's topics are trivial. Women will claim guys just don't get what is important (relationships around them). Guys will complain women get too myopic and that being interested in celebrities gives a bigger picture. While these generalities on topics are repeatedly discovered in communications research, it should be noted that they are not very important when dating because typically the participants are so interested in the other person that they are willing to sit through less interesting conversations to get to know the other person better.

What you discuss on a first date should vary and feel natural, but you might want to have a few topics or questions reserved in case the conversation has a hard time getting started. Topics to discuss on a first date typically will be confined to the first few levels of intimacy as described in Chapter 3 to include cliché, facts, preferences and opinions. While you may have some conversation strands that reach into the values and hopes and dreams stages, be careful not to delve too quickly into these more intimate conversations.

Light Topics/Questions for consideration:

Where have you lived? Where did you like best? Why?

What schools have you attended?

Do you have any siblings/what was it like growing up in your family?

Past or present work

Favorite media (movies / music)

Mutual friends (but don't gossip)

Favorite pastimes / hobbies / sports

What inspired you to go on this date?

What do you see as a next step in life?

Funny stories of childhood

Who has been the biggest influence in your life?

What kinds of things make you laugh?

What's your favorite place in the entire world?

What were you like as a kid?

Do you have a nickname? What's the story behind it?

Who was your favorite teacher/professor/college course? Why?

What do you hate most about the dating process (so I can avoid it!)?

What was the last book you read?

What's your favorite book? Do you relate to the main character?

Do you have any pets?

What's the best part about your job (or major, if in college)?

What's the worst part about your job?

What's the most interesting thing you did this week?

What do you like best about your friends? (Bonus: this will tell you a lot about what they look for in a relationship)

What charity would you donate to or volunteer for?

Do you have any artistic talents?

What do your parents do?

What were you like in college/high school/middle school?

Are you the same as or very different from how you were as a child?

Have you ever met anyone famous?

Do you think politics are boring or interesting?

Most people enjoy being asked questions about themselves and will be flattered that you are interested in them. Whatever you plan to ask, be ready for the question to be flung right back at you, often as a prerequisite for them to answer the question. You must also ensure your date has your undivided attention, possibly even turning off your phone or other distractions to let your partner know they are important to you. As with every amorous excursion, a man should display loyalty to his lady friend by only having eyes for her and not letting his natural search for beauty get him distracted by other women. A lady should likewise not look at other guys too much, or talk about another guy too much, because most men don't appreciate thinking they might have competition. Jealousy is a poor foundation for relationship.

One more thing to note about light conversation is that the goal is to listen more than it is to be heard, and the most impressive conversationalists make everything about the other person. Talking serves a purpose and can be fulfilling, so your goal is to fulfill the other person's need to talk rather than concentrate on fulfilling your own need. I remember receiving an award at the U.S. Embassy in London, and the ambassador's wife went from person to person just asking insightful questions and making everyone in attendance feel important and right at home, even though clearly the most important people there were the hosts.

This can be particularly difficult for men, so let me give some very specific advice. When she says she had a hard day, it is your job to sympathize with her, not to tell her how yours was worse. When she says she had a victory celebrate it with her rather than trying to one up it with a brag. Treat her stories as more important than yours. The Bible instructs us to, "Rejoice with those who rejoice; morn with those who mourn" (Rom. 12:15). Your job is to let her have the emotional tone of the conversation, and show you are interested in her life.

This also leads to a warning. People who don't feel good

about themselves often can't let others feel good about themselves either. These people tear down accomplishments instead of offering praise, and criticize instead of accepting good news. If this is repeatedly evident in conversations realize that your partner may be struggling with envy and self-loathing and they are probably not ready for a long-term romantic commitment.

Bringing God into the Relationship

You might have noticed that none of the above "light" questions involve spiritual matters. For Christians, I would guess nearly every first date will include some discussion of spiritual things, but I think these discussions should come up in conversation naturally and not be forced or discussed without context. Furthermore, a wise person will already be somewhat knowledgeable about the other's religious background even before accepting a date. The Bible is very clear about how believers should not be "unequally yoked" in marriage to nonbelievers, and our obedience to this command starts with our dating habits (II Cor 6:14). Dating evangelism is to be avoided, and even differences of Christian background (Catholic vs. Protestant) or theology (Wesleyan vs. Calvinist) can create serious divides later in the relationship.

When discussing spiritual things, be sure to try to understand not just the other person's beliefs, but also their activities. What spiritual disciplines do they follow (fasting, praying, Bible study attendance, reading the Bible, memorizing scripture, praying, etc.)? Do they have a spiritual head/authority? To whom do they look for spiritual guidance?

To whom are they accountable? Obviously these are all personal questions and should not be asked in a grill- session; these queries will typically come up a little later in a relationship.

Many people have also asked me about appropriate spiritual intimacy before marriage. My answer usually surprises them. I do not think couples should get too involved spiritually before marriage primarily because I think it is too personal and can lead to premature physical intimacy. Furthermore, the man doesn't have spiritual authority over a woman until they are husband and wife, so the spiritual union really begins at that moment (see Eph 5).

Before marriage it is thus important to worship beside each other rather than as a couple in isolation. You should spur each other on to good deeds, church attendance, relationships with mentors, and going on retreats. Observe your partner as they worship in community, and be on your guard if they are so individualistic that they reject spiritual authority or try to have it over you before marriage. Though some may think it is shallow, I also would be cautious if my potential future mate did not sing during worship time. A Christian should enjoy the spiritual communion with God found in singing His praises, and no lack of singing skills should be able to overcome the Psalmist's exhortation to make a "joyful noise" to the Lord.

Some spiritual activities you can enjoy before marriage include memorizing the same scripture and holding each other accountable to it or reading the same devotional book and scriptures and then discussing your life lessons. You certainly can pray together in public, but I think you should avoid making plans for extensive prayers in private. By all means attend church together and other religious activities, but try not to be so distracted by each other that you do not gain the full benefits of the activities you are attending. It is vital that you have a spiritual life apart from each other, for it is in that space that God can most easily speak to you if you need to be warned away from the relationship.

Perhaps one of the best things you can do is participate in group ministry together, either at a local ministry such as a soup kitchen or on a missionary team in another culture. These types of activities may tell you a lot about what the other person is made of as they suffer some hardships and are forced out of their comfort zones.

More Serious Dates and Discussions

After you have been dating for some time, you may wish to start moving the relationship toward marriage by having deeper conversations and more intimate dating experiences. Some ideas include going camping with responsible friends or parents or doing outings with your parents, your partner's parents, or maybe even both sets of parents. You can also plan more detailed extensive excursions such as going on longer trips together, but try to be prudent so as not to put yourself into any situation that has extreme temptation.

In my own experience, after dating for a few months events conspired to have me attend the Defense Information School in Maryland while Rebecca stayed in Washington State for a few months. While apart (and calling each other every night!) we had a burst of inspiration and decided to plan a trip across the United States from Maryland to Florida and then back all the way to Seattle. This seemed adventurous, and Rebecca figured it could be a real test—after all, if she could tolerate me for that long in a small car she might indeed be able to tolerate me for life. It was on this trip that we had our first kiss (on the Empire State Building) and that we eventually expressed our love for each other for the first time.

I do not think this plan would be prudent for most couples as there is too much temptation being on your own for extended amounts of time. The way we did it was to plan the whole trip so that we only slept at family and friends' houses. One day we had to drive 18 hours straight to get to our next resting place, but we were determined to only stay with other people instead of being alone. In this manner we avoided staying in a hotel room together and thus avoided both actual sin as well as "the appearance of evil" (I Thes. 5:22).

One couple I talked to said they had a similar long trip when they were engaged and that they did stay in the same hotel room (different beds). They succeeded in being morally pure by enacting the "hand shake rule": they agreed to shake hands before entering the room then not to touch each other in any way until they left the hotel. I have also heard of people putting a Bible prominently between the beds to ensure separation. While mature Christians who put in place wise boundaries may succeed with such policies, in general we should abstain from all circumstances where we might be heavily tempted to cross our moral boundaries. The devil is good enough at tempting us without our putting ourselves in morally precarious positions.

One common "morally precarious position" is ending dates by "parking." I remember in high school I took my date to the drive-in theater and discovered that I paid little attention to the movie and much more attention to her. Lucky for me we didn't go too far, since later that night her dad knocked on our door and laughed at the fact that he had taken his wife to the same movie we had chosen. We should be wise when dating and protect ourselves when we are most vulnerable. That would especially include being in the dark, being somewhat tired late at night, being alone, and certainly if you have been drinking alcohol or some other inhibition-lowering drugs (which, of course, I'd greatly discourage you from ever having).

On more elaborate "serious" dates you may wish to move the conversation out of more superficial topics and toward things that are deeper and more meaningful. Here are some potential topics and questions.

Topics for Deeper Relationships:

When did you accept Christ as Savior and Lord?

Have you had any personal revelations about God

What you want to do in life / career plans?

What you find interesting/fascinating in the other person?

Moments that shaped your life

Past relationships

What should I know about you that I'd never think to ask about?

Favorite memories

Most embarrassing moment (only if you're willing to
    share yours)

Do you think your name fits you? What about my
    name?

What did you think was "cool" when you were about
    7 years old?

Is there a band you used to love but can't stand now?

What was the best night of your teenage life?

What did you want to be when you grew up when you
    were a child?

What are you best at?

What do you think of (insert political issue here)?

The goal is to get to better know if this is the person you
will chose to love for the rest of your life. You should listen
carefully to their answers and analyze those answers as best
you can. To assist you in that process here are some ways to
analyze various deeper questions.

How would you describe yourself as a small child (under 12)? (Their self image)

This question is disarming because they think it is only
about the past, but you should keep in mind that what they
remember being as a young child is much the way they still are
today, or at least the way they perceive themselves to be. If you
see a large disparity between their past and present, ask them
about it—what shaped their life, and what caused them to
change? If the description seems accurate for the present, you
may consider asking them if they feel they have changed in any

particular regard. Try to guide the conversation so that it reveals their self image, and be careful if you unveil a person who is wounded or hurting or damaged in some serious way. While wounds may be endearing when dating (most people are pleased to help heal others), if they are deep enough, they might prove difficult in a long-term relationship.

What did you learn about women (or if you're a man, ask about men) growing up? (Their opinion of the opposite sex)

Many times the lessons we learn about the opposite sex as children and that spring to mind from this question are more fundamental and will characterize how the other person will see and interact with you. If the answer puts your gender in a positive light, that is good. If it puts your gender in a negative light you may need to probe further to see if the notion lingers or if it has been greatly modified by time.

My personal reply would be that I didn't learn much since I grew up in a family of four boys, and pretty much my mother had a great influence on what I thought about women. This might indicate that I am inexperienced and maybe not heavily opinionated yet. It would certainly mean that I was heavily influenced by my mother, making it rather vital that you get to know her better to understand me and my perspective about women. If my mother were strong, effeminate, opinionated, shy, or heavily into the "woman's liberation movement," you can bet that would color my view of all women. I personally am grateful that I gained an excellent example of what a woman should be from my mother.

How would you describe either of your parents? (How they will treat you)

This question has two benefits. First, it will show you which parent was most influential, as typically they will pick that parent to describe. Second, many people say that one of the best indicators of how you will be treated in a relationship is to see how your partner treats his or her parent of the opposite sex. If she is a spoiled "daddy's girl," she'll expect you to spoil her too, or if he is verbally aggressive with his mother, he will most often also treat you that way in a long term relationship. Try to understand if they respect their parents, because that indicates a good background and the potential for wisdom.

You may also expand this question by asking which parent they are most like or by asking them about what failings they see in their parents. Try to discover if your partner is overly critical or if they are grateful for the good characteristics they have inherited. You may also want to discover if your partner shares poor traits or if they have overcompensated in a certain area due to their parents' influence or failings.

What are your siblings like? (How they are at keeping relationships)

Having brothers and sisters greatly expands a person's development and understanding of both themselves and others. Whereas being an only-born child usually helps develop a sense of responsibility, having siblings often involves learning cooperation skills. Birth order is discussed at length below, but here it is important to note that solid relationships with siblings can mean your partner is used to working through problems and performing relationship maintenance. If he or she has poor relationships with all his or her siblings, it might indicate a failure to respect others or to expend effort in keeping relationships. It may also indicate a person who "burns bridges" and may be prone to do the same to you. If he or she has a poor relationship with a sibling who is the same gender as you, you may also take that as a warning sign and wish to discover the source of the relationship's malaise to see if it indicates anything that could turn out to be detrimental in your own relationship.

What's the difference between your ideal and real self? (Personal weaknesses)

This is a thinly disguised version of the dreaded job interview question "What are your weaknesses?" People will often tell you what they least like about themselves, and you'll be tempted to disagree with them and tell them they are not that way at all. Still, carefully consider what they say. If they give you a non-answer, it may indicate that they are not good at self-monitoring and that they do not recognize their own weaknesses. If they say they are their own ideal it may indicate a person with a large ego. The best situation is when they bring up something that indeed is a weakness and they confess it then explain how they are working through it. This is most encouraging because you want to marry someone who can see his or her own flaws and will expend effort to change rather than someone who is blind to his or her own flaws or who thinks he or she is already perfect.

For me, success in life would involve_____ (Life goals)

This question is fun because your partner will often flounder around wrestling with how to describe success. Though it is basically an impossible question, listen to see if the goal involves personal attainment of a desired career or goal or if it involves relationships and being satisfied with life. The book of Ecclesiastes has a lot to say about success in this life, but its conclusion could be summed up by 1 Timothy 6:6 which says, "But godliness with contentment is great gain." Success and satisfaction are not destinations so much as they are journeys.

I do not feel we are made to be satisfied in this life or to feel "successful." Indeed, it would be foolish for God to optimize us for this life when we will soon be in eternity. He has chosen to optimize us for our true identities and occupations, which will only be revealed after death when we receive our new identities in Christ (Rev. 2:17). This can create frustration on earth, because people who do not know God scrap and claw trying to be powerful here without understanding that we were meant to be so much more in the eternal realm.

We must therefore define success as living our lives not for ourselves but for others and specifically by living our lives for the glory of God. Our lives have an audience of One: if He is pleased we have been successful. It doesn't matter what you do in life; you can be successful regardless if your job was

President or submarine sewer cleaner as long as you do everything for the glory of God (I Peter 4:11).

What was your last embarrassing experience?

When you ask this question, look for the physiological signs of embarrassment, including lip pressing, blushing, and averting the eyes. All these signs indicate that the other person still regrets the incident, and cares what other people think. According to Dacher Keltner, researcher of positive emotions at the University of California Berkeley, embarrassment is a "moral emotion" that shows humility, modesty and a desire to make peace. Blushing is therefore a good sign that the other person feels regret, and so may have learned from their previous antisocial behavior. Keltner admits that if he had to chose a wife by speed dating, this is the question he would ask. He would then watch for the typical signs of embarrassment, and if those were not seen he would he be able to strike another name off his list. If you want a spouse who cares what other people think, who wants to follow the rules, then you had better pick a person who shows embarrassment rather than always looking "cool."[61]

As you have these discussions, pay attention and try to detect any areas that need more probing or where your partner may be misleading you. One of the best indicators of deception, or at least indicating an area that needs more exploration, is extended pauses for what should be easy questions. This is because the mind has to both figure out the real answer as well as consider a false answer and its potential ramification and attempt to encode the lie so it can be remembered in the future. This is most obvious in kids as when you ask them point blank if they are lying, it takes them an extra second or two to deny lying. Deception can be indicated by touching the face, displaying incongruous emotions, and true answers leaking through nonverbal gestures (repeated shrugging or head shaking "no" while saying "yes").

Trust your intuition, especially if you are a woman. The other day my wife Rebecca was guiding us to a house we had never seen, and I asked her if we had male-type directions or if we were relying upon her feminine intuition to find the place. In response she asked which I'd rely upon more. Though I was betraying my own gender, I wisely answered immediately that I'd rather rely on her intuition. Often intuition, especially in a woman, is a good guide in relationships.

The Birth Order Discussion

One of the most informative questions you can ask is what siblings your partner has and try to understand what role each sibling played in the family hierarchy. Similar to Chapter Two's discussion on the attractive characteristics of similarity and complementarity, birth order is a powerful determinant of personality characteristics and can be used to better understand your compatibility with a mate. Dr. Kevin Leman explains in *The New Birth Order Book*[62] that each child added to a family alters the family structure, so that each child is in effect born into a slightly different family than the former child. This means children can be categorized as only borns, first borns, middle borns and last borns, and each of these types are predisposed to certain personality traits.

Only born and first born children are generally the "straight-laced" types who follow rules, like to lead and make decisions, and generally work hard to become successful. When they were younger, they benefitted from doting parents and when they grew older they learned responsibility by taking care of their siblings. These individuals tend to be opinionated decision-makers who are confident in their decisions and seldom see things from other people's perspective. Often they turn out to be aggressive movers/shakers in business or very attentive nurturers in the home.

Middle born children get less attention and learn to compete and negotiate. They are natural born peace-makers and bridge-builders, who are typically good followers and tend to be very loyal. They get the least space in photo albums and often the least attention in families, so they may develop a kind of loner streak. Often they will choose to excel in areas the first borns do not: if their older sibling is good at sports, they tend to choose academics and vice versa. Second borns are motivated to keep the peace and often wish to please others. Having more than one middle born, however, may result in having a "black sheep" in the family as they learn they cannot compete with the elder siblings so they don't try to excel at anything and often get into trouble.

The last borns are the babies of the family who quickly learn that it takes serious work to get attention. They often expect to be cared for and will go to serious lengths to get attention. For them, rules exist to be skirted if not outright broken, and what matters is pursuing a good time. Because they always had someone to bail them out, they tend not to worry about consequences but will often jump into things without much forethought. They are often the most personable of the personalities and can be great salesmen and comedians.

Of course the above descriptions are only generalizations of the theory, and birth order characteristics are greatly nuanced by other factors such as personalities of parents, years between children, and gender. If the parents are overly critical, it can wipe out many personality traits and create resentments in children that outweigh other factors. If there is a spread of 5 years between children often the traits will reset. For example, my wife is the last born but is five years younger than her closest sister and thus mostly has first born characteristics. Finally, gender can have a huge impact since the boy who has older sisters will often be pushed into having more first born traits, and the middle born only girl with five brothers may be spoiled and pick up some last born traits.

You may be asking what all this has to do with finding the person of your dreams, and the answer is: "A lot!". According to *The Birth Order Connection*, you should never marry someone who has the same birth order as yourself[63]. In fact, for two first borns or two only borns to be married seems to be a recipe for divorce. At the very least it often results in many opinionated conflicts with little backing down or resolution. Two last borns in marriage often results in a kind of chaos with no one taking charge and no one willing to make the necessary hard decisions. The least problematic pairing of the same birth order is two middle borns, who when married will seek peace but will also have difficulty making decisions and may bury differences and feelings to the point of creating something that looks more like a truce than a marriage.

If you want financial security, marry a first born who will aggressively pursue life and generally follow the rules to get ahead. The problem is you cannot expect such a person to give you too much of their time, because they are out trying to individuate (remember the term from chapter 1). You may also find that the firstborn has too many rules, and expects others to follow their lead without question.

Middleborn are extremely loyal and can make great mates for both first born and last born, and depending on the exact dynamics, they might also be able to marry another middle born. They "…tend to have the lowest rate of infidelity of all birth orders[64]," but they are less predictable and even tend to be more secretive than other birth orders. If you want a generally peaceful union, middle born are best, but you may also find life less exciting or successful than marrying other birth order types.

Marrying the last born works well as long as you are willing to spend time with them and make them feel special. They will often "spice up" life for other birth order types, but they tend to want everything to be positive and have unrealistic expectations. As a general rule they tend to jump into relationships too fast, are able to manipulate relationships to make them what they want, and they tend to be the first to leave a relationship if it isn't constantly measuring up to their idyllic expectations.

So what are the best combinations? According to Dr. Leman, the best is only born with youngest, then first born with youngest, then middle with youngest. Avoid marrying someone with the same birth order and instead look for someone who shares your values (especially religion), intelligence level, money habits, ambition level, and passion level.

One more note on how to analyze birth order. If possible, marry someone who has opposite gender siblings. Psychologists realized long age that one of the reasons marriages have tension is that people simply don't understand the opposite gender. As my son with three sisters can attest, there is no better education about the opposite gender than growing up with them.

All of this wisdom about how to have conversations will do you little good if you do not act on it. Albert Einstein once said, "Men marry women with the hope they will never change. Women marry men with the hope they will change. Invariably they are both disappointed." You are far wiser to wait for the right person than to think you will change your spouse over time to become the person you want them to be. If you cannot accept them now for who they are, you are better off not trying to develop a relationship hoping to eventually change them.

This chapter has given you some ideas for dates and many ideas for topics to discuss in order to really know your significant other. In the next chapter we will continue to explore important conversation areas and give tips so that you know if you should commit or resolve to dissolve the relationship. We'll look at the main topic areas that result in divorce, discuss some red flags in relationships, and give you some ideas to further explore your compatibility and lay the foundation for a love that lasts a lifetime.

CHAPTER NINE FURTHER LEARNING

1) What questions here do you like best and want to remember to ask on your next date?

2) What are some good dating ideas in your local area?

3) Describe your favorite date so far. What made it special?

4) What is an ideal date for you?

5) What do you think is a good limit on spiritual integration before marriage?

6) How do YOU define success in life? How do you define success in love?

7) What characteristics (especially birth order) in a spouse would make a perfect match for you?

8) What birth order should you most try to avoid?

CHAPTER 10

Knowing Good Fruit from Bad Apples:

Marriage or Break-up?

"Love has nothing to do with what you are expecting to get—only with
what you are expecting to give—which is everything."
— *Katharine Hepburn*

God recognized that it was not good for Adam to be alone, so He gave Adam the task of naming all the animals with the hope that Adam would find "a suitable helper." Adam must have marveled at God's extensive and ingenious creation like scientists and enthusiasts still do today. He also must have felt pleasure to participate in God's creative act, using his own creativity to generate appropriate names. This must have been a monumental task not only due to the number of animals roaming the fecund earth but also due to the difficulty of creating names with little experience of animals. Adam was lucky God miraculously had them all line up for him to name, but it seems reasonable that the task took some time as Adam studied them to discover the perfect name for each creature. I would expect that there were many onomatopoeias and names inspired by the animals' characteristic behaviors.

While Adam must have concluded the task with a greater knowledge and appreciation for the nature he was placed on earth to govern, the naming exercise failed in its primary purpose to quell his desire for companionship. God intervened, miraculously removing one of Adam's ribs to create Eve, and thereby for the first time (that we know of) created something from something else rather than creating from nothing. Man and woman are linked from creation, intended to be one flesh.

Adam immediately calls her "woman" because she came from man but only later names her "Eve" (meaning "life") because she would be the mother of all humanity. Adam's claim for her has been proven true by modern science as tracing lineage through the mitochondrial DNA has proven that all humans alive today share a common female ancestor[65]. Adam's decision to accept Eve as his lifetime love was rather easy, given that he knew God created her explicitly for him and that there really were no other options.

Many of us wish the decision to marry would be that easy. We want God to tell us whom He created for us to marry and make it obvious (without necessarily reducing the other gender to just one survivor). As expressed in chapter 4, some people believe there is just one perfect partner meant for you, whereas

I believe there may be a few very compatible partners, but either way the difficulty lies in finding that special other person and knowing it so that you can get engaged and marry. This chapter will help you decide if you have found the right partner, discussing how you can know the other person is the right one for you, pointing out some serious red flags to consider first, and helping you make the most of your engagement time by building a communications bridge that will serve you well the rest of your lives.

How do I know I should get engaged?

Though I started the chapter saying God gave the naming exercise in the hopes that Adam would find a suitable helper, we must also acknowledge that God knew the quest would ultimately fail. This suggests that maybe the whole search for the right one was not really about finding the right one but was a lesson for Adam to better understand what he wanted in a mate. Is it possible that we go through relationships not just to find the right person but also to allow God to work through them to grow us so we are ready to meet the right life partner? Maybe the painful relationships and breakups of the past are necessary for us to know how precious the right person is so we will be ready to commit when we find the right one.

Alternatively, maybe Adam was not yet in the right place to meet Eve, and the search matured him so that he would cherish Eve and she would appreciate him more for the deeper person he had become. Before getting engaged, you should ask yourself if you are in the right place for marriage. Have you matured to the point where you are ready to place someone else's needs above your own? Sometimes time alone is all that is needed as the divorce rate for 21 and 22 years olds is twice as high as for 24 and 25 year olds[66]. You should ask yourself if you have enough experience in life as a single person that you are ready to find your suitable help mate, and you must be certain you are called to marry rather than to be single for life.

Making the choice to love one person for life can be difficult. One thing you can do is ask yourself if you are capable of self-sacrifice on behalf of your romantic partner. If love is a choice, can you easily choose it for them? While love is always a choice rather than an emotion, during the preliminary stages of a relationship the choice to sacrificially love should be fairly easy because it is supplemented by natural emotions. Over time, the need to choose love seems to grow whereas the emotional support to make that choice ebbs and flows. In any case, at the beginning of your life together self-sacrifice should not be too hard to do.

Choosing to sacrifice means wanting the highest good for the other person and believing you are a part of that good. I knew I was in love primarily because I couldn't fathom Rebecca would benefit by being with anyone else more than by being with me. I was so willing to strive for her joy that I couldn't imagine anyone else succeeding in that task better than I. Indeed, I remember thinking that though it would cause me pain, I'd be willing to let her be with someone else if they could be better for her because what I most wanted was her joy.

It should be obvious that we are not talking about "benefit" only in a crass material way. I certainly didn't have much money to offer Rebecca. Giving of yourself often is more difficult than spending money. You must be certain that you'd give anything for the other's betterment, that you are ready to sacrifice yourself on their behalf, and that you do not consider the sacrifice on their behalf to be sacrifice but instead you feel it is a foregone conclusion. If the answer to the question "What makes you happy?" is not "him" (or "her") but rather, "Whatever makes him (or her) happy," you have strong evidence that you're in love.

I also think that you should be crazy for the other person. I'm betting this was not what you thought a Christian book would say, but I have found that this principle is indeed a great metric to help determine if the other is the right person. Far too many relationships seem to get stuck in a phase where one of the partners has no "sizzle" for the other but simply sees nothing wrong with the relationship and therefore has no reason to discontinue it. This is what happened in one of my own relationships before Rebecca. I could discover no real reason to break up with my first girlfriend and no good reason not to get engaged to her, yet after a few years of dating, I realized I wasn't crazy for her either, though I was very attracted to her physically. The interpersonal "sizzle" had calmed to a simmer, and that is a bad sign at the start of a life-long relationship.

I wish I could sit down with you and really help you ask the right questions as you struggle to decide whether or not to make a relationship permanent, but in the end the decision would still be yours. The fact that you are reading this book suggests to me that more than 80-90% of the people out there are not good enough for you. Don't sell yourself short. Marry someone who has what you want. Save yourself for someone you find irresistible, who excites you, and whom you'd be glad to serve the rest of your life. Find someone you can be passionate about, you can trust with your life, and whom you respect. Marry the man or woman who has captivated you by romance, who sincerely loves you more than they love themselves, and who will be a good parent for your children.

Many couples say at some point they realized they could not imagine living without the other person, and that is how they knew they were in love. This sentiment may be emotional-based, but it is so common that I feel it is also a good way to know that you are in love.

Finally, one point you may have expected is that I think before getting engaged you should have a confirmation in your heart. You don't need to hear the actual voice of God (though many do), but you do need His peace about the decision. The first person you should tell that you are getting engaged is God, and ask Him what He thinks about it. I know many Christians rely too much on getting supernatural experiences from God while others deny that it is even possible. In my experience, God can be sensed (often we say "felt"), and I think this level of decision is important enough for Him to break into our natural world with His supernatural presence. God's touch doesn't have to be earth-shattering, but the decision to be engaged should "feel right." Many people I have counseled or couples we have met have expressed that they felt the Lord's confirmation, and that touch stays with us to encourage our marriages as well.

Having proffered advice on how to know when to get

married, let me also offer some essential wisdom to assist you in this process. The number one problem with determining if you are in love is an overdeveloped physical relationship because it makes you feel obligated toward the other person, and you cannot differentiate between sexual attraction and life-long attraction. If you allow your physical intimacy to go too far, you'll find it hard to know what is emotion and what is your will, and you'll discover that it is much harder to know God's will since you have sin hurting your relationship with Him. Your understanding of your own heart will also be impaired because you will have chosen physical pleasure above the best for the other. While physical intimacy "just feels so right," it is actually very harmful to you both, and thus going too far sexually is a sign that you are not loving self-sacrificially but instead have comingled elements of selfishness. You must not make a life-binding decision in a state of sin and apart from close communion with the Holy Spirit.

The need to remain pure is easily evidenced by the statistics on cohabitation. Today it has become acceptable in some circles to live together outside of marriage, and some movies go so far as to suggest that you are imprudent not to "try on" the relationship before committing to it. However, only one out of six cohabitating relationships last three years, and only one in ten lasts five years or more[67]. The bottom line is that every failed cohabitation makes you less fit for a lifelong partner, and living in sexual sin will impair your ability to make a good decision about getting married.

Red Flags in Eden

Before you ask her to marry you, or if you are a lady before you start hinting that he should ask you the big question, carefully consider some "red flags" that have proven warning signs for people in the past. While one warning flag might be enough, a combination of signs should tell you that for your own good you must end the relationship.

Watch out for people with violent tempers or volcanic anger. Anger by itself is fine, especially if directed at evil, but if it erupts almost uncontrollably, it is very dangerous and suggests a person who needs more work from the Holy Spirit. Look especially at why the person is getting angry—what started it, and can they control it? If it is due to selfish needs or wants or appears to be beyond the other person's control, proceed only with great caution.

You might also consider a lack of patience as a warning flag, as lack of patience is one of the easier ways to see selfishness. Patience involves being able to take not getting exactly what we want when we want it, and your date might show it to their parents, siblings, or the poor waiter who is doing his best to work on a busy Friday night. If your date gets angry at small inconveniences, he or she may also easily get mad at you in the future.

Having patience has even been linked to success in life. One study at Stanford[68] in the 1970s observed six-hundred four-year-olds who were told they could eat a marshmallow immediately or, if they were patient for 15 minutes and didn't eat the marshmallow left in front of them, they could have two marshmallows. The struggling children employed various tactics including cover their eyes with their hands and turning around so that they couldn't see the marshmallow, while others started kicking the desk or tugging on their pigtails. Many of them played with the marshmallow as if it were a tiny stuffed animal, while others simply ate it as soon as the researchers left the room. In the end, a minority ate the marshmallow immediately, many struggled but succumbed to the temptation before the 15 minutes were up, but about one third successfully deferred gratification long enough to get the second marshmallow. Years later it was found that those who had patience at a young age had higher SAT scores, earned more college and graduate degrees, and even had healthier body weights as adults.

Women should especially be careful if their man mistreats other women in any way. Whether it is a mother or sister or former girlfriend, not treating women in a chivalrous manner should be a big red flag since there is a chance that he will eventually treat you that way. Certainly any sign of abusing a woman should be cause for terminating the relationship.

On the topic of abuse, most pastors and psychologists would agree that a person who experienced sexual abuse as a child has a much greater likelihood of becoming abusive. As a general rule, do not date or marry someone who was abused. This rule seems grossly unfair since the person I'm suggesting you avoid was the victim, but there is simply too much evidence that abuse leads to more abuse. At the very least make sure that you know the other person's story, that they have worked through the commensurate issues with a pastor or other counselor, and that you always keep your eyes out for warning signs that they too may be becoming abusive. Often an early indicator of impending danger is pornography use.

While it is often awkward to discuss, knowing about your partner's past relationships can help you identify and potentially avoid some pitfalls. Make sure you know if the other person is "rebounding" from a prior serious relationship and ensure you know why they broke up. If they are dating you soon after a serious relationship, give them plenty of time to fully recover from their past before planning a future with together. Also, try to discover if the other person has a habit of breaking up when things get serious, or even worse, if they have a pattern of breaking up and getting back together with the same person, which both indicate dedication problems you do not want in a marriage. You may also take a partner's inability to commit to your relationship as a warning sign.

The inability to commit is typically portrayed in movies as being mostly reserved for men, but both genders can be afflicted by it. When it is the male, it could be that he is just dragging the relationships on because he is comfortable with it and doesn't want to "put himself out there" to find someone else, or as mentioned earlier in this book he may simply be using the lady to occupy time until he finds "someone better." Most women seem to be able to sense when the relationship is not advancing, and breaking up because a relationship appears to be "going nowhere" is perfectly legitimate. It might even be the exact thing the guy needs to open his eyes to how he feels about the lady and jumpstart his interest in marriage.

Other warning signs include the presence of immaturity, the inability to admit they are wrong and ask forgiveness, and a high degree of selfishness in other relationships. Often they can act unselfish with their paramour, but have a more difficult time trying to hide their selfishness in other relationships. Be careful if your date has wandering eyes watching other people rather than being consumed with interest in you, and don't continue in a relationship in which the other person tries to control you or force you to do things you find uncomfortable.

Sometimes other considerations have a heavy influence on the decision to get married such as education, timing, and finances. While it would be nice to be out of debt and have finances figured out, or to both have graduated from college etc., to me the priority is each other, and the details often work themselves out. Greg Behrendt in his book *He's Just Not That Into You: The No-Excuses Truth to Understanding Guys* wrote, "There will never be a good time, financially, to get married, unless you're Shaq or Ray Romano. But somehow people manage. If your man is using money as an excuse not to marry you, it's your relationship that's insecure, not his bank account[69]."

You may also be warned away from marriage by better understanding your own motivations. Don't marry for revenge or because you are lonely, need security, or want sex. Don't marry because the other person reminds you of a parent or acts the opposite of your parents or because marrying someone will make your parents mad. Don't marry to rescue someone, to please someone else, or just to show world you're lovable. While most of these reasons to avoid marriage may seem obvious, counselors constantly discover these flawed initial motivations when people are struggling to avoid a divorce.

While some people are simply in love with the concept of marriage, never forget that living as a single person is far better than living in a difficult marriage.

Enjoying An Engaging Engagement

When you decide you want to get married, be sure to do the whole process right because there is a good chance you'll tell the tale of how you got engaged many times throughout your lives together. Guys should ensure they do the chivalrous thing by asking the lady's parents for their permission to request her hand in marriage. The lady may need to drop hints that she is willing, dragging the guy into the mall jewelry store to show him rings she likes or showing him a picture of a pretty wedding dress she'd like to wear someday.

Let's assume you have found your life-mate and you have committed to marrying each other. What's the purpose of an engagement? How do we maximize this period of time to best prepare for a marriage?

While some time is certainly needed just to make all the preparations for a great wedding, the time should also be used to wisely prepare for a great marriage. In Biblical times being engaged was close to the same thing as marriage as both partners (and often the lady's parents) agreed to the permanent union. Their purpose in having an engagement period may have been to gather family or to raise the needed funds for a dowry. In the Western world's recent past the betrothal period was needed just to get the two people to know each other better since social mores often prevented young couples from spending much time together unescorted and because often marriages were arranged affairs with little concern for personal compatibility.

In our world the engagement period is the perfect time to lay a foundation for your relationship. I suggest making it no less than 3 months and no more than a year about six months is a good target duration. Your purpose is not just to pick the right cake and send wedding invitations, but also to try on the feeling of being more intimately connected and dedicated to another person. Some people even say that the stress involved with arranging your wedding is the perfect test of the relationship's ability to endure.

One essential component of engagement is getting premarital counseling. Your pastor may be able to it or else he can recommend a Christian counselor. It is even possible to get this kind of counseling in an informal setting from a married couple you both respect, but it is typically better to seek someone who has done counseling before and is trained to help you mature your relationship and spot potential problems.

Counseling will often include taking various forms of personality compatibility tests and will most likely force you to consider some introspective questions as well as discuss the "big six" topics that are most often associated with relationship dissolution. While these activities are best done with counselors, there is nothing wrong with getting a head start on the conversation by considering these activities here.

Personality and compatibility tests are easy to come by these days, with some versions available online, and sometimes partial versions are available for free. The DISC personality assessment tool will help you discover to what degree you possess four personality characteristics: Dominance, Inducement, Submission, and Compliance. Typically your results are graphed on a scale with a vertical axis that ranges from Assertive to Passive and a horizontal axis that ranges from Open to Guarded. While this test is not really geared for amorous relationships, it might help partners understand and appreciate each others' strengths and weaknesses. It is usually best when the two partners do not have identical scores but instead balance each other out in the measured dimensions.

Possibly the most ubiquitous personality test is the Myers-Briggs Type Indicator (MBTI) which measures psychological preferences for how people perceive the world and make decisions. Four categories are measured on dichotomous scales to understand: 1) Attitudes (Extraversion and Introversion), 2) Perceiving Functions (Sensing and iNtuition), 3) Judging Functions (Thinking and Feeling), and 4) Lifestyle (Judging and Perception). This data may help you understand yourself and your partner. While this test is backed by impressive statistical evidence, you still may wish to take the findings with a grain of salt. After all, my Myers-Briggs suggests "personal relationships, particularly romantic ones, can be the INTJ's Achilles heel." My wife and I laughed at this irony since I'm supposed to be a communications and relationship expert.

Myers-Briggs Dichotomies:

Extraversion (E)   -   Introversion (I)
Sensing (S)   -   Intuition (N)
Thinking (T)   -   Feeling (F)
Judging (J)   -   Perception (P)

Though they have less evidence supporting them, there are some organizations using both partners' Myers-Briggs preferences to predict compatibility[70]. I would not put too much credibility in these findings, but they might prove interesting as conversation starters during your engagement.

Once again, the clearest use of these tests is to ensure you do not share many identical traits because that could lead to conflict, and to better understand your partner's personality so you can know why he or she responds in certain ways. The more you know about them the better equipped you will be to appreciate him or her and overcome relationship rough spots. As discussed earlier in this book, you should also know each other's "love languages" and understand how birth order may impact your relationship.

The engagement period is the perfect time to begin growing closer spiritually and lay the groundwork for spiritual intimacy during marriage. Since you have obtained permission from the bride-to-be's parents to get married, spiritual authority starts transferring to the husband-to-be, permitting deeper spiritual interaction. While too much spiritual intimacy still holds the temptation for excessive physical intimacy, hopefully it can be better resisted with the knowledge that you will soon have the much-awaited physical union.

Perhaps the most powerful force on earth is corporate prayer as God promises to hear our prayers and make His presence manifest in our midst (Mat. 18:20). Marriage makes it possible to share many moments throughout the day with a person who can join you in petitioning the Almighty for His will to be done on earth as it is in Heaven. During the engagement period you may wish to start a habit of praying together. Maybe you can pray together for five minutes before you go on a date, or after the date and then migrate this pattern to your marriage by praying together before or after the day. You might also decide to read the same scripture, and maybe study the passage independently then get together and share your findings. Furthermore, you can start practicing other spiritual disciplines together such as memorization and fasting. Perhaps you can challenge one another to fast or go on a specific-item fast for a set time period such as lent. Why not decide to fast a day or three days or even seven days, asking God to bless your future union and be glorified in it?

Your wedding is also very important, and while it is beyond the scope of this book to give you comprehensive wedding advice, here are a few tips to maximize one of the most important days of your life. If possible, hire a professional wedding organizer who has solid recommendations and hire a professional photographer to record your special day. Write out your own vows so that each of you deeply considers exactly what you are pledging to each other in front of God and many witnesses. Make sure you have a fun reception where you can interact with all the family members, and do not cut it short in your haste to start the honeymoon. Finally, remember that the whole day is YOUR day, so if everything "goes wrong" but you enjoyed it, it was indeed a great success.

The Big Six Compatibility Conversations

Essential conversations during an engagement include

talking about religion, sex, children, money, morals, and recreation because these are the topics that most often create stress and division in marriages. You do not have to have identical opinions of these topics, but you do need to be able to live with the other person's viewpoints. For example, if you do not have any recreation pleasures in common, or if you have a lot of libido (sexual energy and desire) and your partner does not, you may be heading for some frustration.

It is by far preferable if you date someone who knows God in a similar way to your own knowledge of Him. These days few people talk very much about theology when dating, but if you get married, you will have to decide what church you will both attend, how to raise your children into your religion, and how to celebrate religious holidays. Do not date or marry thinking you will convert your partner to your religious perspective; while they do not have to agree exactly with your view of God, you both must at least be tolerant of each others' religious beliefs and able to respect them.

Sex is always a touchy subject before marriage, and much of what needs to be discussed should be shared after marriage. Still, while you are engaged, you can discuss your sexual expectations (taboos, frequency, etc.) as well as confess any sexual sins you may have committed. While it is difficult to do, your marriage partner deserves to know the truth, and you should never hold secrets from each other. Furthermore, because in marriage your body belongs in part to the other person, your sexual sins of the past are in fact committed against God, your own body (I Cor. 6:18), and your future spouse (I Cor. 7:4).

There is no need to discuss your sexual fantasies with each other before marriage, and you need to be careful that this topic doesn't lead to temptation. You also should not be worried about your inexperience with sex. Humans have been figuring it out on their own for thousands of years. Part of the fun of a honeymoon is learning how to have sex and what pleases the other person, and inexperience is perfect because then you will not have developed any bad notions. One valuable piece of advice I was given was to take a good Christian book about sex on my honeymoon and read it with my wife. After marriage you must remember that you need to communicate to optimize your sexual relationship just like communication helps maximize other parts of your relationship.

Before getting married it is a good idea to settle on what you feel is the ideal number of children. While the number of course can be flexible as the reality of having children sinks in, an initial understanding may help prevent future heated discussions or outright explosions due to unrealized expectations.

In my relationship we both said we thought we wanted four children, and though that number may have fluctuated as the burdens and joys of raising children became more manifest, we now have four wonderful children. While I would be happy having more, my wife feels we have arrived at the right number, and I am comfortable with that decision in part because my initial expectation was met—any more children would simply be a bonus. Children really are a blessing from the Lord, and I do not feel I would have enjoyed as full an experience of life if I had fewer children.

Many other issues can be raised when it comes to having children. Do you share the same ideas on childrearing? Typically the contentious point here is discipline. While I plan to offer much more guidance on raising kids in a future book, here I will simply say that proper discipline is part of loving your kids well (Heb. 12:6), and you would be wise to have at least a basic understanding on this topic with your future spouse. Other family issues include how you will handle vacations, and what you will do on holidays when both grandparents want to see their grandchildren.

One of the topics that creates stress in every relationship and even tension in some, is how money will be made and spent. To make this discussion practical, consider going over the other person's budget with them and see if you agree with their current expenditures. If they don't have a budget, just check out each other's checkbooks and credit card statements. It may also be very instructive to discuss debt. In general, young couples should avoid debt unless it is in the form of an investment (house, education) or, with more caution, an essential large purchase such as a car. Furthermore, you'd be wise to pay off any debt with a high interest rate rather than start a savings account with a lower interest rate in your favor.

Make sure you discuss who will be the primary wage earner as the other person often must uproot their job and modify their career expectations in order to accommodate the primary wage earner's needs. While I am a traditionalist and think it is best for the husband to earn all necessary income allowing the wife the option of staying at home or working as she wishes, in the modern environment many couples find they both must work to make ends meet. On the other hand, many couples do not realize that one person's income could suffice if they just did away with some of the expenditures such as a second car, expensive cell phone contracts, and cable TV.

Another financial issue is how the money will be stored. I strongly recommend a joint account where both partners can see all expenditures and thus hold each other accountable. If you want some money separate and unseen from the other person (maybe to use as a personal allowance or in buying presents for the spouse without them knowing), it is very easy to transfer money to a debit card rather than to set up a separate bank account. The goal is to understand that the money is held in common and should be spent together as well, though allowances can be made to make the system more flexible as needed.

Morals and values often are based on a religious foundation, but there are some issues that must be discussed regardless of a person's religious background. For instance, what will you do when you both disagree on a serious decision? Are there some ground rules for arguing fairly? Do you believe divorce is an option, and if so, under what circumstances? While I plan to go in depth into marriage relationships in a follow-up book, here it is important to note that in most solid marriages both partners have agreed that divorce is not an option. Divorce should not even be considered by either partner, and if your mind does go there, it should be a warning to seek external assistance. In fact, considering divorce may be an indicator of a failing union, and often this mental consideration reveals itself in a verbal threat. Treat any talk of divorce seriously and seek immediate assistance to rebuild the relationship.

A final topic for discussion is recreation. Often young couples just love being together and do not consider the need for long-term activities that provide mutual enjoyment. How compatible are you in the area of having fun? Do you share a love for a certain sport or card games or hiking? While you can have individual hobbies that the other person does not enjoy, you ought to have at least some diversions in common. If you do not, it might be time to try each other's pleasure activities or look for something new you can start together.

Recreation is also related to your future location together. For example, if you like boating or hunting or hiking, it might play into your decision about where you will live. If one of you likes the inner city and the other prefers the suburbs or country, it might deserve a serious conversation. Proximity to family can also be important as it is recommended that your first location be a two hour drive from the nearest family member, but when you have kids, it is nice to be in the same town as the grandparents. These days most people simply go where they can find a job, but it is good to discuss these issues in case you do have options.

Back to Eden?

Many couples cannot imagine difficulties in their future marriages, but this very blindness can be a liability. It's vital that you do not set expectations too high but instead reasonably realize you will not always be perfectly compatible.

You may disagree at times, you may hurt each other, and you will argue sometimes, but the key is loving through it and growing through it. Marriages are not built of brick and mortar but of love, forgiveness, and the willingness to be a good best friend. The little things are important, as you lean toward each other each day. The best marriages include many small favors, quick hugs, and fond eye contacts.

This advice is similar to that ultimately proffered by Dr. John Gottman in his book *The Seven Principles of Making Marriage Work*[71]. Gottman teaches at the University of Washington and has a 92% accuracy rate for predicting divorces after couples spend just a day in his "marriage lab"[72]. He claims the main indicators of divorce are criticism, contempt, defensiveness, and withdrawal. Criticism involves attacking a partner's personality or character, usually trying to prove them wrong and often using generalizations such as "You always…" or "You're the kind of person who…" Contempt is attacking a partner's sense of self with the intent to insult them, often name-calling or using sarcasm. Nonverbal contempt involves using a sneering tone of voice, eye-rolling in derision, and curling an upper lip in contempt. In this context defensiveness means always seeing oneself as the victim, making excuses rather than accepting advice, and meeting a complaint with a complaint of your own rather than accepting responsibility. Often defensive people use the phrase "It's not my fault…" and repeat themselves rather than paying attention to what the other person says. Finally, withdrawal involves being emotionally removed and unresponsive, and acting like nothing is wrong when something clearly needs discussion.

Gottman gives some communication advice to overcome these dysfunctions, suggesting couples learn to make specific complaints and requests rather than use generalizations, try hard to listen and understand partners, and show them respect by validating their good points. When trying to talk through an issue, you should claim responsibility and even ask your partner, "What can I do differently in the future?" Defensive personalities must learn to rewrite their inner scripts, replacing thoughts of righteous indignation or innocent victimization with thoughts of appreciation and responsibility. Finally, do not let yourself ignore an issue or withdraw from conflict emotionally but instead engage in conversation. If you need an hour to cool off or gather your thoughts, ask your partner to wait an hour, but be sure to return to the discussion and work through your issues.

One of my first realizations after I got married was that I was selfish and that I got my way a lot rather than giving into other people's wants. Since I am a very persuasive and verbal person, and I came from a home that enjoys verbal riposting, I wasn't used to arguing with a person who is soft spoken and prefers to avoid conflict. While she had to learn to speak up and not withdraw, I had to learn to change the way I argued and be less overbearing. I learned to stop making absolute statements that required her to acquiesce or argue and instead go out of my way to insist she give her input into decisions or her side of arguments. I'm certain that this whole process made both of us better people and that we are stronger together and more in love now than had we not gone through growing pains in our marriage.

Marriage is not meant to be about perfect bliss on earth—it is not a return to Eden—but it does help us navigate the pains, thorns, and thistles of this world on our journeys to the next. I strongly feel marriage is a training ground for us to learn to love as God loves us and that the lessons we learn in matrimony are not intended to stay there but are in fact to eventually be extrapolated to a world that needs examples of real love.

Though they suffered some strong opposition, I am encouraged to consider how Adam and Eve's marriage endured. Imagine the relationship after being expelled from Eden. They lost paradise, were cursed with daily hardships, and just went through a pretty hurtful ordeal. Adam failed as the spiritual leader, standing by watching while Eve was deceived by the snake and disobeyed God's command not to eat of the fruit from the tree of the knowledge of Good and Evil. Adam blamed his own sin on Eve, and even tried to pin some of it on God by prefacing his excuse with, "The woman *you put here* with me…" (Gen. 3:12, italics added).

While many marriages have broken from much less stress, not to mention the future pain of having one son kill the other, we have every reason to believe Adam and Eve's relationship endured for their whole lives. Their union produced many offspring and resulted in seeding the human race on earth. No matter what comes your way, no matter how low culture may stoop, no matter what the future holds, your relationship can endure too, if you build it on a solid foundation and decide to give your spouse a real love that lasts a lifetime.

CHAPTER TEN FURTHER LEARNING

1) What are your vices (so you can find someone who does not struggle in the same areas but instead balances you out)?

2) What red flags do you see in your relationship? Have you asked others about any potential red flags they may see?

3) What discussions do you think are important to have before marriage?

4) Which of the "big six" conversations do you think is most important? Rank order then and compare your list with your partner's list.

5) What spiritual habits do you want in your marriage?

6) What expectations do you have for marriage? Are any of them unrealistic?

7) Why do you think your marriage will last "'till death do us part?"

APPENDIX I

And There Was Light: Small Answers to Big Questions

"Gravitation is not responsible for people falling in love."
— *Albert Einstein*

Included here is a selection of questions I have been asked, often written anonymously, during relationship seminars. Many of them deal with sexual issues, so some readers may wish to keep a higher level of innocence by not reading them. However, since these questions are repeatedly being asked, I feel it is important to address them. It is far better to get biblically-informed guidance than to rely on secular advice in these areas. Some of these questions are addressed in greater detail in the book but are included here to allow a more succinct reference and to help those readers who will never read this whole book but who do have specific questions. These answers are intended to be brief, so readers may wish to get more comprehensive answers from other sources.

Is masturbation wrong?

Scripture doesn't specifically address the issue of masturbation, so we must try to draw upon scriptural principles and reason to understand a Biblical position. While admittedly this makes the answer slightly less credible, it certainly doesn't mean the answer has no credibility. For example, abortion is also not mentioned specifically in scripture, but the two scriptural principles of A) we are knit together and alive in the womb and B) murder is wrong at any age lead us to the natural conclusion that abortion is wrong.

For masturbation the main principles have to do with not lusting after others and that sex was made for couples not individuals. Jesus states, "You have heard that it was said, 'You shall not commit adultery'; but I say to you, that everyone who looks on a woman to lust for her has committed adultery with her already in his heart" (Mat. 5:27-28, NAS). Most masturbation involves imagining nudity or looking at pornography, both of which are clear acts of lustful looking.

I have received the follow-up question of, "What if we do not imagine anyone but simply do it with no visual stimulation?" To address those cases we must remember that we are told to avoid sexual immorality and impurity, and for most Christians masturbation would be included in one of these commands. Masturbation is dangerous because it can be addictive and it can lead to other premarital sexual experiences. Furthermore, it supports the ideology that sex is about taking rather than giving to a partner.

While the evidence suggests masturbation is not an acceptable Christian practice, I hasten to say that sexuality is God's glorious gift to us and that we are not forbidden from self-exploration. However, far too often this is also just an excuse to pleasure oneself, and certainly the excuse of "self-exploration" cannot be used more than for a single occurrence. In general, it is best if you do not practice this at all, and certainly you should follow the Lord's leading through your conscience.

Many objections have been made to this "masturbation abstinence" advice, so let me briefly address the most popular one. Contrary to popular cultural advice, there is no physical need to masturbate—the body does not require it and millions of people live single lives without it. Most of the other objections are likewise just excuses to try to continue doing something based on "it feels good" rather than on sound principle.

Do I need to repent from a "wet dream" (orgasm during sleep)?

Repentance involves turning from sin toward purity by asking for forgiveness and deciding to act differently in the future. Often wet dreams occur because of thoughts contemplated or pictures viewed while awake, and if this is the case, then you can repent and change your waking patterns to better "take captive every thought to make it obedient to

Christ" (II Cor. 10:5). However, if there was no sin in the waking hours and the wet dream happens without your conscious intention to contemplate sexual things, then there is little you can do to change, and thus real repentance is not only unnecessary but also impossible. Erotic dreams can happen regardless of intentions or level of waking purity. Thus, if you need to change your awake lifestyle, then by all means do so, and if you feel guilty about it (or anything!), by all means repent with the firm conviction that God will hear you and forgive you of all unrighteousness (I John 1:9). On the other hand, if you have good habits of mental purity while awake, the dream was really beyond your control, and you do not feel guilty for it, then it probably doesn't require repentance.

At what point is virginity lost?

Strictly speaking, virginity has to do with having had no intercourse. However, I think the word loses most of its significance if a person has done "everything but" intercourse. Sadly, the church has often given the concept of virginity too much emphasis when the real issue is purity. You can lose purity without losing virginity. Virginity can be thought of as purity without knowledge, and since it involves innocence, it can only be had once and lost once, making it a precious gift to your future spouse. However, with God's forgiveness everyone can have purity, even after carnal knowledge, and it is purity that is most important. Many sexual acts other than intercourse cause you to lose purity. While you can never regain innocence or virginity, you can regain purity (see the next question about that).

Sometimes this question is posed because people are wondering if having oral sex means losing your virginity. Oral sex is most certainly still sexual intercourse and results in loss of innocence and purity. Indeed, in many ways it is more dangerous than normal sexual intercourse, since mouths have more bacteria and can get and transmit STDs. It is a lie from Satan to suggest oral sex is an acceptable alternative so that you can keep your virginity (see the answer below on oral sex in marriage).

How can I be made pure again/is there redemption after having had sex?

You cannot be innocent again, but you can be pure again, and sexual purity is the real issue. Never forget that while the Old Testament speaks of all God's creation as being "good," the New Testament is mostly about how He sent His son to earth to fix the "good" that had been lost. The big word for it is "redemption". There are serious ramifications to sexual sin such as sexual disease, sinning against our own bodies, hurting present and future relationships, potential pregnancy, etc. God's grace is more than sufficient to cover it all in His love and forgiveness. I John 1:9 states, "If we confess our sins, he is faithful and just and will forgive us our sins and purify us from all unrighteousness" (NIV). Sexual sin is just one more sin that Jesus died on the cross to take away. The worst thing you can do is to refuse God's free forgiveness, in effect judging yourself and scorning God's love. Remember that your worthiness has nothing to do with His forgiveness. Jesus didn't die for people's sins because they were worthy; He died because it was in His nature to love us and bring glory to the Father by acting on that love. We are even told that receiving forgiveness somehow betters us because those who have been forgiven much love much (Luke 7:47).

There is nothing that can separate us from the love of God (Rom 8:39). Your sexual sin is already paid for in full, and forgiveness is waiting for you. Jesus has taken your sin and paid it in full on the cross. Once you give it to Him in repentance, it is no longer yours, but now it is part of your boast about what God has done for you. God is in the business of redemption, and He's good at His business and does it completely. If you're ever tempted to feel guilty, take captive the thought and exalt in the truth that Christ has redeemed you. You need to resist guilt from the devil if you've given the sin to God. You may regret the sin, but you do not need to feel guilty for it now that Christ has taken it away.

You should also put in place boundaries to ensure you do not fall for sexual temptation again. Often it is much more difficult to resist sexual temptation after you have failed to do so once, so you want to be very wise and very careful who you date. You should also read the below answer to the question, "How do you resist sexual immorality?"

How in-depth should you talk about sex/wedding night with your future spouse? (Also: When is a good time to talk to your significant other about sexual issues?)

This topic is discussed earlier in this book, but in general there is no need to discuss wedding night activities before you are engaged, and even then there is little need for the discussion since part of the fun of a honeymoon is learning how to pleasure your partner physically. The danger with having sexual discussions prematurely is that talking about sex can lead to temptation, so if you must do it, try to talk about it in a public place when there is no chance that you will be alone immediately afterward. A better plan is to save the deeper sexual discussions for the honeymoon when the temptation will be appreciated and your desires can be fulfilled.

Before you are engaged you should limit discussions on sexual topics. The only sexual topic you should discuss is your sexual past, because it is important that you both know what you are getting into and the potential difficulties that could be involved. Hiding past sexual sins is unfair to the partner, and your relationship isn't ready to progress unless you are both comfortable having no secrets between you.

After you are engaged and closer to your wedding date, you may wish to discuss contraception as well as expectations for the wedding night and sex in marriage thereafter. Often guys are obsessed with frequency while women are more concerned with practical issues such as "Will it hurt when the hymen is broken?" or "What if I can't make him happy in bed?" (which there is pretty much no need to worry about). The answers to these questions and many more can be found in a good Christian book on sex such as *The Act of Marriage* by Tim Lahaye or *Intended for Pleasure* by Ed Wheat, which I suggest you wait until your wedding night to begin reading.

Your best move would be to discuss your sexual questions with a good mentor or one of your parents. Pretty much anyone you respect who has been married and you trust may be a good source. Even if you are too shy to do this and have little knowledge about sexual matters, there is no cause to despair—people have been figuring it out for centuries, and the wedding night is just the beginning of years of exploration and learning how to enjoy your partner physically.

Why do men believe women do not have sexually impure thoughts?

Men probably have many more sexual problems than women because men can more easily treat sex as an act rather than a relationship, and they are more tempted by sight alone rather than needing touch to get excited. Statistics clearly indicate men are far more prone to have adulterous affairs than women, and they are more likely to treat the affair as being temporary rather than wishing it to become a long-term relationship. Still, it is not true that women are spared sexual temptation and problems; they are increasingly prone to succumb to pornography. More than 20% of pornography viewing is now done by women. An added danger for ladies is that they can more easily generate impure thoughts from written words, and they seem attracted to unrealistic fantasies that are manifold in culture in the form of soap operas and "chick flicks." It is good for us all to realize that women are also tempted in this area, and need to flee sexual immorality and take captive their sexual thoughts.

How do you resist sexual immorality?

There are many things you can do to resist sexual immorality, and you should be encouraged to know there still are many people who are virgins when they get married. The first and most obvious thing to do is remove the temptation either by refusing to put yourself in a compromising position (parked car late at night) or by actively changing your surroundings (get controls on your Internet service, refuse to watch sexually suggestive programs, etc.). In general, sexual temptation seems to build upon itself, so rather than thinking that pornography will serve to lower your temptation, you should realize that in fact it raises your interest in sex and makes it seem more acceptable rather than being the sin it is. Pornography further degrades the sexual act and teaches sinful and selfish sexual activities, so for your own good it should be avoided.

Second, you can get accountability. Meet with someone at least once a week who will ask you the tough questions, pray with you, and make you realize that your sin will not go unnoticed. Third, be sure to daily pray and memorize the Bible. Jesus defended Himself against temptation by using Scripture (Mat. 4:4), and you can wash your mind using God's word. Furthermore, prayer not only results in God working more powerfully in your life, but it also makes you acknowledge His presence at all times, often making you stay away from temptation.

Fourth, if it is a big temptation for you, consider fasting and adding consequences for failure. Fasting shows God how serious we are and develops discipline that can be used to resist temptation. If we can resist food, which is essential for our bodies, we can resist sex, which is not. You might also consider having a policy that makes failure in sexual areas more punishing. This might involve not allowing yourself to spend time with your significant other for a week if you break a boundary or having to pay money to the church when you fail. The idea is not to equate our punishment as paying for our sin, but to drive home the seriousness of our sin. Most young people I ask confess that they would think twice about touching someone in an inappropriate place if they knew they would be fined $100 for the act. Too often we set an awfully low price on Christ's saving blood.

Fifth, the Bible clearly instructs us to "take captive every thought" (II Cor. 10:5), and this is indeed where the battle should be fought. It is not sin to be tempted, but it is sin to tempt ourselves by letting our thoughts play with the temptation. Do not dwell on evil but put your minds on things above (Col. 3:2).

Finally, one principle of spiritual warfare that has proven very effective for me has been to let sexual temptation remind me to pray for someone's salvation. This allows me to get on the offensive instead of only playing defense. The idea is that one demon is tempting me while others are trying to ensure a friend doesn't come to Christ, so if I let my temptation remind me to pray, those demons may fall into conflict with each other. In any case, I find being reminded of eternal salvation lessens my temporary physical temptations.

How do you resist lust when it is for the person you are going to marry?

The answer is pretty much the same as given above with the added incentive that waiting for marriage is also good for the person you love. Your self-control can help them remain pure. Sex is not irresistible, and your love for a person may make you want to engage in sex, but it should also help you resist it, knowing sex will harm the relationship and cloud your understanding of God's will for the relationship. Remember that resisting your significant other sexually is building trust in your future marriage because if you can resist him or her sexually, he or she can trust you to resist others when you are married. This is one reason returning to abstinence is so important if you have sinned sexually—you still can reap many of the benefits of abstinence because it will show your partner that you are serious about sexual purity and you have the willpower to resist.

If I made a commitment back in middle school to not go past holding hands, but I didn't know what I was committing to, do I still have to honor that commitment?

Many well-intending churches and Christian leaders are going far beyond biblical instruction to create borders that will ensure our overly sexually-stimulated society doesn't get the best of us. Are our immature commitments to God or others still binding? Scripture warns it is better to not make a promise than to not keep our promises to God. At the same time, we recognize that minors cannot make legally binding agreements and that even adult agreements can be nullified if we didn't have sufficiently accurate information when we made them.

I think immature commitments can be discussed with God and your parents who are your spiritual authorities and who have your best welfare in mind. Do not throw out all boundaries but instead discuss how you wish to establish a more appropriate boundary. If your spiritual authority agrees and you do not feel God is pressing you to keep the former boundary, then you should proceed under the new boundaries.

If I'm dating someone who has sexual sin in their past, what should I be most concerned about when considering marriage?

This is a great question, but it is difficult to answer it in a way that is general enough to apply to all situations. You would be wise to first consider if this relationship is in God's will as a partner with previous sexual sin suggests he or she may be weak in this area and therefore may be more prone to pressure you toward sex outside marriage. If his or her sin was not just out of wedlock but of a sinful nature (homosexual, bestiality, child abuse, or sex with a family member) then you would be wisest to immediately terminate the relationship.

The key in these relationships is to set clear and solid boundaries since the other person proved weak in the past and sex is so addictive. You furthermore must insist they have no ongoing sexual-related sins such as pornography viewing, which also serves to increase temptation. Finally, and this is often the most difficult part, you should insist that your partner get tested for STDs and that you see the report of clean health. You should have all the details and know exactly what you are getting into before you get engaged or married. Feel free to blame the testing idea on this book—say you read a book and it said this was required and so you'd like them to be tested.

Since you only want to date/court a person you may marry, you need to realize that if you become the spouse, the sexual sin was in part committed against you, so you need to be able to forgive it. If you can't, don't marry them, and if you can't marry them, you shouldn't be dating them. If you can get over it, it still doesn't mean there will be no other consequences that can range from sexually transmitted diseases (STDs) to the need to prove their fidelity before you fully trust them. While I have not seen too many problems involving comparing sexual partners, things like that could also arise and so you must be willing to seek Christian counseling for whatever problems arise.

Where do you draw the line on being honest with your girl/boyfriend/fiancé when discussing sexual sins of your past or present?

First, I sense some ministry needs to be done here since the word "present" was added. If you have sexual sins in the present, get rid of them NOW! Those will make temptation in relationships more difficult to flee and will inhibit your ability to decide whom you should marry.

Second, if you are engaged and have not revealed your sexual sins, you are basically trying to deceive your partner. They deserve to know in general terms what sexual sins you have committed before you are married. You then can ask them if they want to know specifics, and you can give some of them but do so in a tasteful rather than lurid manner. My wife and I both know each other was a virgin when we got married, but we knew it is important not to keep secrets from each other and so during our courting we discussed all our physical encounters with other paramours. You do NOT want to enter marriage without confessing any and all sexual sins. Sexual infidelity before marriage is sin against God, your own body, and your future partner who deserves your life-long fidelity and deserves to know all about you before deciding to dedicate his or her life to joining yours in marriage.

Is "nonsexual" nudity in art the same as pornography?

You should consider it pornography if it incites you to lust, and all such material must be avoided. This certainly includes Hustler or Playboy but may even include Victoria's Secret "non-nude" catalogs or even the pictures on the walls in the underwear section of your local clothing store. Unfortunately, these days even commercials, PG movies, and trips to the beach may include people sufficiently unclad to tempt you or at least to act as a gateway to make you want to seek more temptation. The Bible instructs that we guard our hearts and minds and be careful what we view. Let us all know ourselves and avoid whatever content creates lust within us. Jesus said, "But I tell you that anyone who looks at a woman lustfully has already committed adultery with her in his heart. If your right eye causes you to sin, gouge it out and throw it away. It is better for you to lose one part of your body than for your whole body to be thrown into hell" (Mat 5:28-29). While the last sentence can be seen as hyperbole, the warning is clear—it would be better to be blind than give in to looking with lust, which can lead to sin. Since that is the case, it should inspire us to even radical behavior to keep our eyes and hearts pure.

That being said, when it comes to the fine arts there seems to be some room for individuality. I remember nude statues or paintings used to cause me to think sexual thoughts, and I was tempted to stare at the body parts that were revealed. I therefore wisely chose to never stare but would look away when I saw explicit material. I remember thinking it was strange that people allowed such content just because it was oil on canvas rather than a photograph. Interestingly, now that I am older (and married) I am less tempted in this way, and I can appreciate the human body as fine art in many cases without feeling sexual temptation.

At the same time, not all fine art is equal—some of it is obviously intended to be prurient. Thus, when it comes to fine art, we should first guard our own purity, and we should think twice about whether our judgment of a work applies to others. In the end it is probably wisest to treat fine art as a "disputable matter" with specific guidance given for us in Romans 14.

I have heard of people "channeling" their sexual drive into ministry. Can you speak to that?

Strangely enough I have heard of a guy who made this exact claim, and he later had a sexual encounter with one of his students in the high school group. This is a silly thing to say and an even worse thing to practice. No, you cannot really "channel" sexual energy into ministry, and people who say things like this should be looked at with careful scrutiny as it probably means they are struggling sexually. Instead of "channeling" the energy they need to get counseling and possibly withdraw from ministry until they have their lusts under control.

Of course, it greatly depends on what exactly a person means when they use such a nebulous phrase. If it means the person is staying busy in ministry and service and so has less time to be tempted, i.e., their lust is lowered and under control, then I suppose it could be acceptable. I do not, however, believe it is wise to have someone who is truly struggling sexually in a leadership position over opposite-gender youth who could be exploited.

Do you believe God has picked out a spouse specifically for each person, or does He give us wisdom to choose for ourselves?

This issue is covered more deeply earlier in the book. I think free will and choice are assumed human qualities from Genesis to Revelation and that part of being human is making real "free" choices. God created us with choice so that we could grow into His image by choosing to love. It is not free will that God necessarily values, but it is love, which can only be done if we have free will. Ultimately God is in control and can intervene in any way He pleases, but typically He allows us to chose and live with choices so that we can mature.

When it comes to finding a future marriage partner, I think your choices are limited but real. They are limited specifically to believers, as the Bible says we should not be "unequally yoked" (II Cor. 6:14). Never date or marry a non-Christian. You are also limited by your location and preferences. This limitation is being overcome with technology as 12% of all marriages are people who met online first.

I think God has quite a few people who may be optimal for you. Some of them might be optimal because they compliment you and spur you on to godliness; others may be more contentious but still drive you to God and make you a better person. I think you do not need to be too concerned that you may miss the "right one" because another "right one" could come by at any moment. At the same time, we need to be VERY careful not to date the wrong ones. While I think Rebecca and I have had a great marriage for more than 15 years, I think we each could have had similarly pleasant experiences with someone else, that is, with another Christian surrendered to God's will. Thus, I think there is no "perfect" one for you so much as that there are a few "best ones" who are "best" in different ways.

Is oral sex normal and permissible in Christian marriages? What acts are not allowed in Christian marriages?

There are a wide range of teachings here both because scripture does not seem perfectly clear at times due to translation and cultural issues as well as because people like to justify their own actions more than they want to discover God's will for their sexual union. I used to be extremely conservative, and I still recommend that position as a default because it has few drawbacks. Still, it seems wise to know exactly what the Bible prohibits during marriage so that we never cross the intended line.

For most of my life, I thought the Bible prohibited oral sex since the English word "sodomy" means oral and anal sex.

Indeed, up until recently (1960s) both of those sexual acts were illegal in all 50 states. However, I found it curious that in the Song of Solomon there are possible references to oral sex, and they seem to be celebrated. One passage requests the "lover" to come into the lady's garden and "taste its choice fruits" (Song of Solomon 4:16, NIV). Thus, when I learned Hebrew, I researched the word and discovered that in Hebrew "sodomy" is only talking about anal sex. Oral sexual contact is nowhere specifically prohibited in scripture.

My general suggestion is to not practice oral sex until you have been married for some time and are both comfortable with each other. If one of you feels it is wrong, you should respect that. In some ways it does seem a bit dirty, in that you are putting your mouth where urine comes out. Realize also that mouths have more bacteria than genitals, so STDs are also more of a concern. In fact, something as common as cold sores are actually Herpes simplex 2 and can be transmitted into genital herpes by simple contact.

Some sexual activities are wrong at all times, including during marriage, and God detests them so much that they incurred the death penalty in the Old Testament. These include anal sex, bestiality, and incest. Other things seem obvious perversions of the sexual drive, such as sadism and masochism in which violence and sex are intermingled and thus should be avoided.

Whatever you do, keep in mind that sex is about culminating physically your relationship's love. It is about giving to the partner, not taking, and about being united with them, not being lustfully selfish. I do not think all role playing is bad, but some of it should certainly be avoided, especially if one partner is trying to imagine themselves with someone else. Lingerie or costumes do not seem unhealthy, and while sexual toys or creams, etc. seem rather unnecessary, I do not see a scriptural reason for forbidding them.

Sadly, sexual mores are changing rapidly in America, and soon nothing will be considered wrong by the culture. Just like in Rome, our sexual values will continue to decay from strong family values to permitting sodomy and possibly eventually even legalizing pedophilia and bestiality. The culture's moral decay should not sway Christians who know God is the creator of sex and that His laws are right and for our own good.

How far is too far when dating? Is kissing and hugging before marriage a sin? What does it mean to "follow your conscience in sexual issues?"

These are good questions that deserve a more complete answer, so please read chapter 5.

How does the way women dress affect guys?

Men are very attentive to visual stimulation, and it takes a lot of effort not to look twice at a shapely lady. Our culture increasingly produces styles that are sexually suggestive, and young women are encouraged to be "sexy." Not only does this create a mentality that prefers outward appearance to inner beauty but it can also stimulate sexual thoughts in guys that can result in pornography use later in the day. While the woman is not guilty of causing the sin—it certainly was the man's poor choice—a godly women should avoid being in a stumbling block for guys struggling to remain pure. Paul in the Bible specifically gives guidance in this area saying, "I also want women to dress modestly, with decency and propriety, not with braided hair or gold or pearls or expensive clothes, but with good deeds, appropriate for women who profess to worship God" (I Tim 2:9, NIV).

The crux of the instruction is that Christian ladies must dress modestly and value inner beauty over outer appearance, while the specifics such as "braided hair" may be seen as related to Paul's time period. The most obvious cultural difference between his time and ours is that "braided hair" was often a sign of prostitution. It might also have been a sign of excessive concern for looks, even as is rampant today. In Biblical times, women hired *ornatrix* (hair dressers) to spend hours piling their hair high like a tower[73]. These hair dressers also applied cosmetics and determined the proper complementing jewelry to include earrings, collars, trinkets, pendants, bracelets, rings, and even circlets on ankles. Paul's exhortation to do good works is not only approbation against flaunted wealth but also a practical injunction to save time.

Why is sexual sin so easy to fall into?

I'm convinced sexual temptation is calibrated at the perfect level between too much to resist and too little to care enough to procreate. The real problem is that our culture has placed sex everywhere, making temptation ubiquitous. Imagine if everywhere you looked you saw and smelled great food—it would be very difficult to resist becoming a glutton. Sexual temptation is found everywhere, so our desire for it has been exacerbated.

The key is therefore to lower sexual messages in your life. As a teenager I realized sex was a dangerous temptation, so I cut out songs that were too suggestive. We should limit our intake of movies or TV or music or whatever has sexual references so that we are less tempted.

Is it normal to not desire sex, even a little bit?

It may not be normal for an adult, by which I mean the average person's experience, but it need not be dysfunctional either. Some people are called to be single for life, and a lack of interest in sex might be part of that calling. It could also be that you have other more important things in your life that take precedence right now or that you have successfully removed the more temptation-laden elements of our culture from your daily experience so you do not feel the pressure like many other people do. In general, if you feel low on libido before marriage, you should feel blessed. On the other hand, if you have been sexually abused or other circumstances have occurred that may have led you to lack a sexual desire, you would be wise to seek counsel and work through some issues in your past so that you can best please your future partner.

Why are all men/women alike—they are all _____ (insert derogative)!

I agree that it can be difficult to find the right person to marry, and it may be true that everyone you date behaves the same way, but you must realize that the common denominator in all these relationships is YOU. Often we are attracted to a certain type of person, and if that type is hurtful you may wish to look inside yourself to see what it is that attracts you to this type of personality. We often see brokenness in others far better than we see it in ourselves. If you are in a pattern of dating people who all mistreat you in a similar way, seek counseling and try to learn what it is in you that attracts these others and why you find them attractive. The best way to change the character of the people you attract and date is to improve your own character. As pastor Andy Stanley likes to say, try to become the kind of person who the person you are looking for is looking for. Better yet, become more like Christ and you will attract people who are more Christ like.

Is there wisdom in trying out the relationship sexually before marriage? Has science discovered any disadvantages to our "hook-up" culture?

There is no need to "test drive" your sexual desires for each other, and a large part of the fun on a honeymoon is discovering details about your own desires and how to meet those of your partner. As mentioned earlier in the book, people who cohabitate have a much higher rate of divorce, and all sexual activity outside of marriage is forbidden by the Bible. This prohibition is because God designed our bodies and sex and wants them both to be used for maximum long-term enjoyment which can only be found in a dedicated marriage.

Science is confirming the Bible's teaching that "casual" sex outside of marriage is damaging. The feminist sociologist Lisa Wade performed a qualitative study of 44 freshman students and discovered that most of them were, "overwhelmingly disappointed with the sex they were having in hook ups." This was true of both men and women, but was felt more strongly by women. Having "casual sex" was found to disempowered people. A 2010 study by Carolyn Bradshaw of James Madison University found that only two percent of women strongly prefer the hook-up culture to a dating culture. Miriam Grossman in her book *Unprotected* recounts how women long for emotional involvement with their partner after a hook-up, and that 91 percent of women experience regret, 80 percent of women wish the hook-up hadn't happened, and 34 percent of women were hoping the hook-up developed into a relationship. Furthermore, a 2010 psychology study out of Florida State University discovered that students who have casual sex experience more mental and physical health problems, to include eating disorders, alcohol use, stress, depression, and suicidal feelings[74].

If you want to get the most out of marriage, don't worry about your sexual performance but instead spend time getting to really know your partner and practice selfless love for him or her. A great sex life in marriage will naturally spring from a great interpersonal connection, and you can work on that kind of connection before marriage.

I am living with my boyfriend and I want to get married but he says his parents were divorced and that marriage just causes strife. He says he loves me, but that we don't need rings to prove it. What should I do?

A real man can commit for life, whereas a boy wants to have some of the benefits of marriage without experiencing the a true life-long loving marriage relationship. You can complain to him all you want, but you should realize that he is not going to change unless you deliver an ultimatum. You must tell him that you want a lifelong relationship and not an extended fling. The only way you can do this is if you realize that you deserve someone who loves you enough to commit, and that he is lucky you haven't left him already.

I furthermore encourage you to see that living in sexual sin is not a good choice for you or your future. The right thing to do regardless of his willingness to marry you is to immediately repent and move into separate houses. God loves you and has a plan for your life, but you will not realize it if you choose a life of sin instead. Furthermore, as discussed in this book, having a period of sexual purity during engagement builds trust into your marriage. Please also see the question immediately preceding this one on live-in situations.

What do I do if I feel like I have married the wrong one for me?

While I hope to write a follow-up book entitled *Adam and Eve Meet Marriage* that will more fully address these kinds of questions, I realize this is a pressing question people have after reading about the way marriage ought to be and comparing it with what they are now experiencing. Let me be clear: God hates divorce, and the second you married and pledged life-long fidelity before God and other witnesses, your paramour *became* the right one for you. There is no other. Your spouse is the right one, and your feelings are incapable of nullifying that truth.

The good news is that God is in the business of redemption—rather than requiring perfection from the start, He heals brokenness and can fix your marriage. If you are not satisfied with your relationship it is incumbent upon you to partner with God and make it right. Start with prayer, add reading good Christian books on communication and marriage, and then throw in some Christian counseling. If possible, partner with a solid Christian couple to see love modeled in action—have them over for a weekly game night or go on double dates. Start renovating your marriage, and watch how God respects your dedication and empowers you with His love and wisdom. Just as a scar is stronger than the original skin, so God often will build in added blessing if you stick with it through adversity. Do not give up on love, for the One who is love never gave up on you.

ABOUT THE AUTHOR

Peter A. Kerr is the Program Director and Assistant Professor of Communications at Asbury University in Wilmore, KY. He is also President of KerrCommunications, providing world-class communications training for marketing, media relations, crisis planning, intercultural communications and leadership improvement. He holds degrees from the Air Force Academy, the University of Washington, and Asbury Theological Seminary.

Peter is an ordained minister and has been published in many places including the books *Adam Meets Eve* and a chapter in *Understanding Evangelical Media,* as well as in numerous magazines and academic journals. He has also appeared on TV programs such as *Marriage Unleashed* as well as *Character Matters.*

A world traveler, Peter has been to more than 50 countries on six continents and speaks various languages. He's worked with many media outlets including *CNN, NBC, FOX, BBC, NY Times, USA Today, NPR, London Times, Der Spiegel,* and *Aljazeera.* Peter led all media relations during the 2004 President Ronald Reagan State Funeral in DC, released the Air Force budget of $120B to the DC press corps, and has media trained hundreds of leaders including White House officials, generals, CEOs, and non-profit leaders. Other experiences include negotiating with U.S. embassies and foreign military leaders in the Middle East, serving as Chief Media Liaison Officer for Outdoor Games in Beijing for the 2008 Olympics, and doing crisis planning for the 2010 World Equestrian Games.

Peter enjoys speaking at conferences and retreats, traveling, reading, playing sports, strategy games, and just being with his wife Rebecca and their four children in central Kentucky.

THE AUTHOR'S TESTIMONY

I accepted God into my heart every Sunday from when I was five until I was seven. Well, I at least raised my hand when the Sunday School teacher asked who wanted to do so (probably greatly inflating their conversion numbers). In any case, when I was seven I was lying in the bottom bunk bed at night and I remember thinking that I loved Jesus and wanted to live my life to please Him, and that is when I really accepted God into my heart. By then I was real good at saying the prayer, admitting my sin, asking forgiveness, and promising to live from then on as He wanted me to live. While I know Christianity is not about feeling but about faith, I remember feeling God's warmth and love enter my life. I then started trying in earnest to live for Him, and began singing to God every night. My mom would sometimes listen outside my door and smile at my amateur attempts to praise God. My older brother in the bunk bed above was less amused, and would sometimes get exasperated enough to come down and hit me. That's why I can say I was persecuted for Christ at seven.

The rest of my testimony is a story about God's guidance and faithfulness. I read the whole Bible by age 12, and haven't stopped reading it. It's truly the word of God, a revelation of our Creator's transcendence and imminence, and if you haven't read it, I recommend you start today! -- Peter

VISIT US ONLINE

If you enjoyed this book and found it helpful, **please** tell others about it, like it on Facebook, and visit our webpage **AdamAndEveMeet.com** where you can read interesting relationship tips and contact the author to discuss speaking opportunities, book signings, etc. Watch for future books by Peter A. Kerr including the sequels: *Adam and Eve Meet Marriage* and *Adam* and *Eve Meet Cain and Able*.

REFERENCES AND ENDNOTES

Chapter One

[1] I do not think God necessarily removes the desire for marriage when He gives the gift of singleness, though He does make the desire bearable. Desires are tricky things, being created by nature and nurture, and able to be changed by both reason and emotions.

[2] Baxter, Leslie. "A Tale of Two Voices: Relational Dialectics Theory." *Journal of Family Communication* 4.3 (2004): 181-92. Print.

[3] "Top 100 Love Quotes." *I-love-quotes.com*. N.p., n.d. Web. 29 June 2012. < http://www.1-love-quotes.com/Top_10_Love_Quotes.htm>.

Chapter Two

[4] Cook, Gareth. "How the Power of Expectations Can Allow You to 'Bend Reality': Scientific American." *How the Power of Expectations Can Allow You to 'Bend Reality': Scientific American*. 16 Oct. 2012. Web. 16 Oct. 2012. <http://www.scientificamerican.com/article.cfm?id=how-the-power-of-expectations-can-allow-you-to-bend-reality&page=3>.

[5] Zajonc R.B, Adelmann P.K, Murphy S.T, & Niendenthal P.M. *1987 Convergence in the physical appearance of spouses. Motiv. Emotion. 11, 335–346*; see also Locke, K. D., & Horowitz, L. M. (1990). Satisfaction in interpersonal interactions as a function of similarity in level of dysphoria. *Journal of Personality and Social Psychology*, *58*, 823–831. ; Folkes, V.S. (1982). Torming relationships and the matching hypothesis. POersonality and Social Psychology Bulletin, 8, 631-636.; Murstein, B. I. (1972). Physical attractiveness and marital choice. Journal of Personality and Social Psychology, 22, 8-12.

[6] Murstein, Bernard I. "Physical Attractiveness and Marital Choice." *Journal of Personality and Social Psychology* 22.1 (1972): 8-12. Print.

[7] Rhodes, Gillian, Alex Sumich, and Graham Byatt. "Are Average Facial Configurations Attractive Only Because of Their Symmetry?" *Psychological Science* 10.1 (1999): 52-58. Print.

[8] Lewis, C. S. *The Four Loves*. New York: Harcourt, Brace, 1960. Print.

[9] Fisher, Helen. "Helen Fisher: The Brain in Love." *TED: Ideas worth Spreading*. N.p., July 2008. Web. 24 Feb. 2013. <http://www.ted.com/talks/lang/en/helen_fisher_studies_the_brain_in_love.html>.

[10] Botwin, Michael D., David M. Buss, and Todd K. Shackelford. "Personality and Mate Preferences: Five Factors In Mate Selection and Marital Satisfaction." *Journal of Personality* 65.1 (1997): 107-36. Print.

[11] Chaucer, Geoffrey. *Thinkexist.com*. N.p., 2011. Web. 22 June 2011.

[12] "Figure 1. Median Age at First Marriage by Sex: 1890 to 2010." Chart. *Census.gov*. U.S. Decennial Census (1890 - 2000); American Community Survey (2010), 2010. Web. 21 May 2011.

[13] Mossop, Brian. "How Dads Develop [Preview]." *Scientific American*. Nature America, Inc., 23 June 2011. Web. 23 June 2011. <http://www.scientificamerican.com/article.cfm?id=how-dads-develop>.

Chapter Three

[14] Keen, Sam. "Top 10 Love Quotes." *I-love-quotes.com*. N.p., 2002. Web. 29 June 2011.   <http://www.1-love-quotes.com/Top_10_Love_Quotes.htm>.

[15] Altman, Irwin, and Dalmas A. Taylor. *Social Penetration: The Development of Interpersonal Relationships*. New York: Holt, Rinehart, and Winston, 1973. Print.

[16] Tarrant, John. "What Is Love?" *About.com*. N.p., n.d. Web. July 2011. <http://honeymoons.about.com/cs/wordsofwisdom/a/whatislovequote.htm>.

[17] Knapp, Mark. *Interpersonal Communication and Human Relationship*. Boston, MA: Allyn & Bacon, 1984. Print.
[18] Lampton, Bill, Ph.D. "How To Make A Strong First Impression: Seven Tips That Really Work."*ThePhantomWriters.com*. N.p., 2004. Web.<http://thephantomwriters.com/free_content/d/l/making-the-first-impression.shtml>.
[19] see more problems with dating in Bradley, Reb. *Dating, Is It worth the Risk?* Fair Oaks, CA: Family Ministries Pub., 1996. Print.; "I Kissed Dating Goodbye" by Joshua Harris; "Dating, Betrothal and Courtship" by Dr S. M. Davis, and "Dating vs. Courtship" by Paul Jehle
[20] Obringer, Lee Ann. "How Love Works." *HowStuffWorks*. How Stuff Works, Inc., n.d. Web. 23 June 2011. <http://people.howstuffworks.com/love7.htm>.

Chapter Four

[21] Dr. Suess. "Top 10 Love Quotes." *I-love-quotes.com*. N.p., n.d. Web. 29 June 2011. <http://www.1-love-quotes.com/Top_10_Love_Quotes.htm>.
[22] Gray, Paul. "What Is LOVE?" Time. Time, 15 Feb. 1993. Web. 1 July 2011. http://www.time.com/time/magazine/article/0,9171,977763,00.html>.
[23] Jong, Erica. "What Is Love?" *About.com*. N.p., n.d. Web. 1 July 2011. <http://honeymoons.about.com/cs/wordsofwisdom/a/whatislovequote.htm>.

Chapter Five

[24] Lopez, Jennifer. "Dating Quotes." *ThinkExit.com*. ThinkExit.com Quotations, n.d. Web. 22 June 2011. <http://thinkexist.com/quotations/dating/2.html>.
[25] While fasting just about anything can be beneficial, the "water only" fast is what was meant by "fast" in the Bible. One false-prophet from the charismatic movement I met bragged

that he was on day 86 of his fast. He looked a little skinny, but not too bad, so I asked him what was in his over-sized coffee container. He replied that it was meat blended with vegetables. To him, anything that was a liquid could be consumed.

[26] Burns, J.R., and R.A. Richards, II. "Love at First Site." *Psychology Today.* Sussex Directories, Inc., 16 Feb. 2011. Web. 14 Nov. 2011. <http://www.psychologytoday.com/blog/repairing-relationships/201102/love-first-sight>.

[27] Helmanis, Lisa. *Master Dating: Living and Loving the Single Life.* Oxford: Infinite Ideas, 2005. Print.

[28] One serious consequence of sexual sin is STDs, with 1 in 2 people having an STD in America by the time they turn 25 (see "Love Facts, Things You Need to Know." *Love Facts, Things You Need to Know.* Real Alternatives, 2010. Web. 01 Dec. 2011. <http://www.lovefacts.org/>.)

[29] "Love Facts, Things You Need to Know." *Love Facts, Things You Need to Know.* Real Alternatives, 2010. Web. 01 Dec. 2011. <http://www.lovefacts.org/>.

[30] I am familiar with the contention that wine back then was not as high in alcoholic content, but that position first of all is admitting that some alcohol is okay, and second loses credibility when the Bible speaks of people taking communion wine and getting drunk—it was not just grape juice being used.

Chapter Six

[31] Ephesians 5:21-28 [21] Submit to one another out of reverence for Christ. Wives, submit to your husbands as to the Lord. For the husband is the head of the wife as Christ is the head of the church, his body, of which he is the Savior. Now as the church submits to Christ, so also wives should submit to their husbands in everything. Husbands, love your wives, just as Christ loved the church and gave himself up for her to make her holy, cleansing her by the washing with water through the word, and to present her to himself as a radiant church, without stain or wrinkle or any other blemish, but holy and

blameless. In this same way, husbands ought to love their wives as their own bodies. He who loves his wife loves himself." (NIV)

[32] Heath, Chip, and Dan Heath. *Switch: How to Change Things When Change Is Hard.* New York: Broadway, 2010. Print.

[33] DeVito, Joseph A. *Human communication: The basic course.* Boston, MA: Allyn & Bacon, 2002. Print. and see also Hall, 1979, 1984; Rosenthal & De Paulo, 1979.

[34] DePaulo, B.M., & Epstein, J.A., & Wyer, M.M. (1993). Sex differences in lying: How women and men deal with the dilemma of deceit. In M. Lewis & C. Saarni (Eds.), Lying and deception in everyday life (pp. 126-147). New York: Guilford Press.

[34] DePaulo, B. M., Rosenthal, R., Eisenstat, R. A., Rogers, P. L., & Finkelstein, S. (1978). Decoding discrepant nonverbal cues. Journal of Personality and Social Psychology, 36, 313-323.

Chapter Seven

[36] Tannen, D. 1990. *You just don't understand: women and men in conversation.* New York, NY: Morrow.

[37] Andreadis, Athena. (February 24, 2013) *Scientific American.* "The 'Language' Gene and Women's Wagging Tongues" in http://blogs.scientificamerican.com/guest-blog/2013/02/24/the-language-gene-and-womens-wagging-tongues/

[38] Sullivan, Andrew. (September, 2000). *Reader's Digest.* "Why Do Men Act The Way They Do?"

[39] Greenfield, Lawerence A., and Tracy L. Snell. *Women Offenders.* Rep. no. NCJ 175688.Washington D.C.: U.S. Department of Justice, 1999. Print. Web.<http://voices.yahoo.com/biological-differences-between-men-women-behavior-7002774.html>.

[40] Wright, John Paul., Stephen G. Tibbetts, and Leah E. Daigle. *Criminals in the Making: Criminality across the Life Course.* Los Angeles: Sage, 2008. Print.

[41] Bilodeau, Sara. "Biological Differences Between Men and Women: How Behavior Is Effected." *Yahoo! Contributor Network*. Yahoo, 29 Oct. 2010.

[42] For a hilarious short video on this topic, watch "It's not about the nail" on YouTube.

[43] Wright, John Paul., Stephen G. Tibbetts, and Leah E. Daigle. *Criminals in the Making: Criminality across the Life Course*. Los Angeles: Sage, 2008. Print.

[44] Larimore, Walt, and Barb Larimore. *His Brain, Her Brain: How Divinely Designed Differences Can Strengthen Your Marriage*. Grand Rapids, MI: Zondervan, 2008. Print.

[45] Weber, Ellen. "Target Differences between Gender Brains." *Brain Leaders and Learners*. Brain Leaders and Learners, 18 Oct. 2003. Web. 2011. <http://www.brainleadersandlearners.com/mita-approaches/target/men-use-logic-women-use-emotion/>.

[46] McGilchrist, Iain. "The Divided Brain." *TED: Ideas worth Spreading*. TED Conferences, Oct. 2011. Web. 8 Oct. 2012. <http://www.ted.com/talks/iain_mcgilchrist_the_divided_brain.html>.

[47] Gur, Ruben C., Faith Gunning-Dixon, Warren B. Bilker, and Raquel E. Gur. "Sex Differences in Temporo-limbic and Frontal Brain Volumes of Healthy Adults." *National Center for Biotechnology Information*. U.S. National Library of Medicine, 12 Sept. 2002. Web. 2011. <http://www.ncbi.nlm.nih.gov/pubmed/12183399>.

[48] Wood, J. L., D. Heitmiller, N. C. Andreasen, and P. Nopoulos. "Morphology of the Ventral Frontal Cortex: Relationship to Femininity and Social Cognition." *Cerebral Cortex* 18.3 (2007): 534-40. Print.

[49] Whitty, Monica T., and Laura-Lee Quigley. "Emotional and Sexual Infidelity Offline and in Cyberspace." *Journal of Marital and Family Therapy* 34.4 (2008): 461-68. Print.

[50] Grewal, Daisy. "Why Interacting with a Woman Can Leave Men "Cognitively Impaired": Scientific American." *Scientific American*. Scientific American, Inc., 13 Mar. 2013. Web.

2012.<http://www.scientificamerican.com/article.cfm?id=why
-interacting-with-woman-   leave-man-cognitively-
impaired>.
[51] Weber, Ellen. "Target Differences between Gender Brains."
Web log post. *Brain Leaders And Learners*. N.p., 13 Oct. 2008.
Web. <http://www.brainleadersandlearners.com/mita-
approaches/target/men-use-logic-women-use-emotion/>.
[52] "Men And Women: The Differences Are In The Genes."
ScienceDaily. Penn State, 23 Mar.2005. Web. 2 Oct. 2012.
<http://www.sciencedaily.com/releases/2005/03/050323124
659.htm>.
[53] Weber, Ellen. "Target Differences between Gender Brains."
Web log post. *Brain Leaders And Learners*. N.p., 13 Oct. 2008.
Web. <http://www.brainleadersandlearners.com/mita-
approaches/target/men-use-logic-women-use-emotion/>.
[54] Fisher, Helen. "The Brain in Love." *TED: Ideas worth
Spreading*. TED Conferences, July 2008. Web. 8 Oct. 2008.
<http://www.ted.com/talks/lang/en/helen_fisher_studies_th
e_brain_in_love.html>.
[55] Fisher, Helen. "The Brain in Love." *TED: Ideas worth
Spreading*. TED Conferences, July 2008. Web. 8 Oct. 2008.
<http://www.ted.com/talks/lang/en/helen_fisher_studies_th
e_brain_in_love.html>.
[56] Fisher, Helen. "The Brain in Love." *TED: Ideas worth
Spreading*. TED Conferences, July 2008. Web. 8 Oct. 2008.
<http://www.ted.com/talks/lang/en/helen_fisher_studies_th
e_brain_in_love.html>.

Chapter Eight

[58] Lachno, James. (May 11, 2011). "Cannes Film Festival 2011:
Woody Allen quotes on sex, love and death." *The Telegraph*.
Web 5 Sep. 2013
http://www.telegraph.co.uk/culture/film/cannes-film-
festival/8507471/Cannes-Film-Festival-2011-Woody-Allen-
quotes-on-sex-love-and-death.html.
[58] Fisher, Helen. "The Brain in Love." *TED: Ideas worth*

Spreading. TED Conferences, July 2008. Web. 8 Oct. 2008. <http://www.ted.com/talks/lang/en/helen_fisher_studies_th e_brain_in_love.html>.

[59] Chapman, G. D. 1995. *The five love languages: how to express heartfelt commitment to your mate.* Chicago: Northfield Pub.

[60] Pausch, R., & Zaslow, J. 2008. *The last lecture.* New York: Hyperion.

Chapter Nine

[61] Cain, Susan. (2012). *Quiet: the power of introverts in a world that can't stop talking.* New York: Crown Publishers. p. 144.

[62] Leman, Kevin. *The Birth Order Connection: Finding and Keeping the Love of Your Life.* Grand Rapids, MI: F.H. Revell, 2001. Print.

[63] Leman, Kevin. *The Birth Order Connection: Finding and Keeping the Love of Your Life.* Grand Rapids, MI: F.H. Revell, 2001. Print.

[64] Leman, Kevin. *The Birth Order Connection: Finding and Keeping the Love of Your Life.* Grand Rapids, MI: F.H. Revell, 2001. Print. p. 24.

Chapter Ten

[65] Parry, Wynne. "Age Confirmed for 'Eve,' Mother of All Humans." *Live Science.* TechMediaNetwork.com, 18 Aug. 2010. Web. <http://www.livescience.com/10015-age- confirmed-eve-mother-humans.html>.

[66] Warren, Neil Clark. *Finding the Love of Your Life: Ten Principles for Choosing the Right Marriage Partner.* New York: Pocket, 1992. Print. p.11.

[67] Whitehead, Barbara, and David Popenoe. "Sex Without Strings, Relationships Without Rings." *The National Marriage Project.* N.p., 2000. <www.stateofourunions.org/pdfs/SOOU2000.pdf>.

[68] Mischel, Walter; Ebbe B. Ebbesen, Antonette Raskoff Zeiss. 1972. "Cognitive and attentional mechanisms in delay of gratification.". *Journal of Personality and Social Psychology* 21 (2):

204–218.

[69] Behrendt, G., & Tuccillo, L. 2004. *He's just not that into you: the no-excuses truth to understanding guys*. New York: Simon Spotlight Entertainment.

[70] *Jung Marriage Test*. 1998. An online test that measures the quality of love relationships. <www.humanmetrics.com/infomate/infomatedemo.asp>.

[71] Gottman, John Mordechai., and Nan Silver. *The Seven Principles for Making Marriage Work*. New York: Crown, 1999. Print.

[72] Gottman, John Mordechai., and Nan Silver. *Why Marriages Succeed or Fail: What You Can Learn from the Breakthrough Research to Make Your Marriage Last*. New York: Simon & Schuster, 1994. Print.

[73] Corcopino, Jerome. *Daily Life in Ancient Rome*. New Haven, CN: Yale UP, 1968. Print.

[74] Smith, Emily Esfahani. "A Plan to Reboot Dating." *Atlantic Monthly*. Nov 5, 2012. Web. www.theatlantic.com/sexes/archive/2012/11/a-plan-to-reboot-dating/264184/